Janet Amare

Soul

**A Practical Guide
For Creating
A Life You Love**

Purpose

Life on Purpose
Publishing

All of the stories in the book relate to real-life people and situations. While some are composites, drawn from the profiles of hundreds of interviews, the names and, in some cases, small details have been changed to allow these people to retain their privacy. If you think you see yourself here, rejoice. It means you are not alone. There are others on the path with you.

Published by Life on Purpose Publishing™
a division of
Soul Purpose Inc.™
P.O. Box 542
Campbellville, Ontario L0P 1B0
CANADA
www.mysoulpurpose.net
Toll Free: 1 (877) 839•2055

National Library of Canada Cataloguing in Publication Data

Amare, Janet, 1958 –
  Soul purpose

  Includes bibliographical references.
  ISBN 0-9688563-0-6

  1. Self realization. 2. Self-actualization (Psychology) I. Title.
BF637.S4A46 2001   158.1   C2001-910441-3

CREDITS
Editing: Wayne Magnuson, *Prairie House Books*, Calgary, Alberta.
Author photograph: Yanka Van der Kolk & Yolanda Van der Kolk Brown, *Power of Self Image Inc.*, Toronto, Ontario.
Dust jacket design: Catina Despotopoulos, *The Cat's Meow Design Inc.*, Calgary, Alberta.
Interior design & project management: Jeremy Drought, *Last Impression Publishing Service*, Calgary, Alberta.

Printed and bound in CANADA by *Friesens*, Altona, Manitoba.

Contents

Acknowledgments

I T seems as though this book manifested itself the moment I was ready to sit still and listen to *my* Soul Purpose. I am grateful to God for inspiring me and creating so much grace around this project. He also provided me with a magnificent team, who read carefully, guided me skilfully, and dressed my words lovingly for market.

I am thankful to Janet Alford for her masterful coaching, and for reflecting to me that I had something of value to say when I was blinded by my healing; Ross Gilchrist, who brought out the *Spiritual Maverick* in me by asking the right questions; Jeremy Drought, my book-builder, who walked me through the intricacies of book design and structure; Catina Despotopoulos, cover designer, who captured the essence with sensitivity and style; and Wayne Magnuson, editor, for caring about the subject and guiding me to simple clarity.

I am indebted to my clients, some of whom are presented here as examples of brilliant pioneers, forging their way towards their purpose. My clients push me to new heights through their courage to heal.

Many good friends inspired and encouraged me: Sarah Rousseau listened to my hopes and fears each week and provided loving feedback that moved me to clarify and take risks; Gerald Parks gave me sensitive ideas to enrich the read; Nancy Henderson graciously supported me in becoming a healer; Lorella DePieri helped me visualize myself as an author; Monica Beattie gifted me with my first writing pen; and Linda Mariani believed in me long before I was even close to my purpose. Thanks especially to Mary Padias; she asked me more often than anyone, "Where's your book?"

My partner, Kathy Walker, radiates a quiet, patient wisdom that kept me in balance. Her love, support and insight through the writing, designing, doubting and trusting have been a great gift. Thank you all for your light.

Janet Amare
Campbellville, Ontario
February 2001

Preface

MY inspiration to write this book has come from the many people I have worked with who have shown me that it is possible to turn your life around, find purpose and meaning, and do what you love. These are the essential ingredients:

- Giving yourself permission—"It is OK to focus on what I want."
- Willingness to change—"It is possible to heal my past."
- Faith—"I have the power to create a great life."

I have been using the information and exercises presented in this book for many years. No matter how often I experience people dramatically changing themselves and their lives, I am still awestruck. It is possible to totally change your life story. You *can* teach an old dog new tricks. We are meant to live happy, fulfilled lives.

The tools and techniques offered in this book are simple, yet the results are profound. I am a pragmatic person—if these steps didn't work, I wouldn't be telling you about them. Everything I offer in these pages I have used myself.

So, how did I learn the steps in *Soul Purpose*?

I started out in a traditional setting, working for the local government, and providing career counselling to disadvantaged groups, such as women, minorities, and persons with disabilities. It soon became clear to me that the natural laws of manifesting were at work in every one of us whether we were conscious of them or not. Just as the consciousness of the scientist affects the test results under the laws of the new physics, the beliefs job applicants hold affect their ability to manifest what they say they desire.

As a counsellor I met many people who shared the belief that the job you get paid for is the one you dislike, while the work you love gets done in your spare time. My greatest gift to others was my own firm belief that everyone can do what they enjoy and earn a good income. As I shared my belief with others I watched their lives change and their prosperity increase.

While working in a traditional setting and evolving through roles in organization development and executive leadership I developed my spiritual connection and saw the manifestations of my personal power. I learned through many teachers that there are universal laws of manifesting and that they work in the practical world.

I began to explore my physical, emotional, and mental health. I learned about, experienced, and then taught about healing that is truly holistic—it affects the physical, emotional, mental and spiritual levels. I realized that there is a process for personal evolution and practical steps to follow, and I used them to create the life I always wanted. Then I began to create ways to transfer these tools of joy and success to others.

I found ways to help people get in touch with their faith in the idea that they have a Soul Purpose. I found ways to assist people in identifying the moments when they feel fulfilled. I developed my capacity to facilitate the healing of issues that keep people from doing what they love. And I created ways for people to learn how to manifest their lives powerfully. This book was written to transfer all this learning to you.

The gift of this book is meant to be one of hope and inspiration. If you know that everyone has a Soul Purpose and that we can all live a fulfilling life, you may have enough hope to dream the dreams that will help you create that life. And, as you read the stories and learn about the transformations that are possible, you may be inspired to do the self-discovery and manifesting work that will get you there.

May you come home to your Soul Purpose easily and with lots of fun.

Janet Amare
Campbellville, Ontario
February 2001

Introduction

SOME people have given up hope. They started out as fresh, passionate young people, full of life, hope and possibility. Then they ventured out into the *real world*.

Somewhere along the line they lost their passion, exuberance, faith, and trust in the idea that they had an important purpose and that it would be enjoyable. They either gave up and left, or gave up and stayed.

There are many *successful* people who fit into this category. They have good jobs, earn a good income, feel well-suited to their work, and yet are sure they are *not* doing their life purpose. What's going on?

We are spiritual beings in physical bodies. In order to have it all—a good income, meaningful work, passion and a sense of purpose—it's essential to create work which links us to our spiritual nature, and at the same time fulfils

> *Many people feel out of touch with their passion and purpose.*

some practical, physical purpose. So, part of the cause of our loss of passion and purpose is our disconnection from our spiritual nature in the way we create jobs.

> *Many people are acutely feeling the loss of spiritual connection.*

At the same time as there is an increase in dissatisfaction with work, there is an increase in the number of people willing to give up the trappings of success for more meaning. They are heading back to nature, cocooning at home, and looking back on their lives to find happiness.

Somehow they are listening more to their insides and connecting with their true spirit. They are more in touch with the truth of their soul, yet they are not sure how to bring it back to the outside world. Rather than recreating their places of work, some are abandoning them and starting fresh.

> *More people are valuing meaning over money.*

The few brave souls who have stuck it out in the corporate arenas, endeavouring to bring more spirituality to the workplace, are wearing themselves thin. The change agents are tired.

We are still short on the critical mass of spiritually-connected people in the workplace. The more people who make space for spirituality in all areas of life, the easier it is to create a workplace where spiritual connection feels possible. We are close to critical mass, and I believe the people of the world are moving towards a more spiritual nature. We are not there yet.

There is another factor that is affecting our relationship with work: *I believe that we are currently living the equivalent of fifty lifetimes in one life.*

In comparison to how much we evolved and changed in one life in the 1800s, we experience about fifty times as much fundamental change today. I believe that this is primarily a soul-level shift, not just the result of increases in technology and mass communication. Our souls are inspiring us, entreating us to move on, evolve, and grow. This puts a huge demand on our capacity to quickly and easily let go of the past and move forward in some new way. We are constantly being asked to reinvent ourselves.

> *I believe that we are currently living the equivalent of fifty lifetimes in one life.*

Many people have learned that letting go means forgetting. They deny their response to change and force themselves to move on, unaware of the bag of emotions that they are dragging along with them. They learn to move on to the next job or life situation as the same person in a new suit. They don't know how to truly heal and transform.

> *Our lives have speeded up. This is not just a result of technological change. Our souls are inspiring us to evolve.*

Most people have learned to reinvent themselves by looking outside first. Which jobs are hot? Who's in demand? Where can I earn the most money, have the most power? Certainly we must be practical, yet if we truly want to feel fulfilled and purposeful we have to do as much research on our inside as we do on the outside. We require a new definition of *work*. *Work is the effort we expend to express our soul in a way that provides a service to others and ourselves.*

Some people have given up on their Soul Purpose, yet more people are seeking purposeful work. Some people are leaving corporations to find meaning, while others are working to change the corporations so they can stay and create more meaningful work.

You need connection to your soul, as well as connection to the world, to create a life that has purpose. Few people know how to balance the two. Our lives have speeded up. We may have ten career tracks in a lifetime and major changes within each track. Change means letting go, and we don't know how. Life purpose means soul connection, but we don't know how to do that and live in the real world.

There are practical tools to connect you with your soul, and they aren't in conflict with living in the real world.

There are practical tools to help you change and heal the past as you reinvent yourself.

You can have your Soul Purpose and have real-world success.

> *There is a way to create and live your Soul Purpose.*

Soul Purpose was written to offer you these things. Here are some guidelines to make the read more enjoyable:

You may want to read through the book once and then circle back to do the exercises. There is information throughout the book to help make the exercises more practical.

Keep in mind that this book is about reconnecting with your soul, healing yourself, and having a great life. These are not small things. You may have some *stuff* come up as you read and do the exercises. In other words, you may bring to the surface some of the baggage you are carrying from past experiences. Please be patient with yourself. Rather than being upset, giving up, or throwing the book across the room, try this: "Oh good, I have some stuff coming up. I'll write down what I'm feeling and use the book to help me process and release the past."

In other words, welcome the issues that come forward. They are guiding you to exactly those thoughts, feelings, and ways of being that must change. If you feel you are not doing your Soul Purpose right now, there are reasons why you aren't there yet. Getting in touch with the reasons is a gift.

The book covers four main components of Soul Purpose:

- Identifying the criteria for the moments in your life when you feel fulfilled. I call this your *"Energetic-of-Soul Purpose."*
- Recognizing and clearing what has held you back from your Soul Purpose. I call this healing.
- Developing awareness and tools to reconnect with yourself. This is skill-building.
- Remembering your natural skills in creating a life you love. This is manifesting.

It takes focus and energy in all these areas to get on track with your Soul Purpose. And, it really *is* worth the effort.

ONE

What Is Soul Purpose?

*"The greatest gift you give others is the
example of your own life working."*

Sanaya Roman & Duane Packer
CREATING MONEY[1]

Does Life Need A Purpose?

DAVID walked in for his first healing session. He sat down and fidgeted nervously. I smiled. Sitting poised on the edge of my chair I made eye contact and held my pen on the pad, ready to write. "So, how can I help you David?" I asked.

He listed three goals: "I'd really like to know why I'm here—what's my real purpose? I've always been interested in music, but right now I'm a tax consultant.

"Secondly, I'd like to have a child. Preferably a cute little boy. That may be tough because I'm not married. I'm not even in a relationship right now.

"And thirdly, I'd like to be wealthy. I'm sure that there must be more to life than what I've experienced up till now. I seem to have been in debt for the last 25 years."

Just as I was about to respond and gently tell David that his order was tall, yet not impossible, he asked one more question.

"Will all this take more than five sessions? I'm on a budget."

Everyone, at some level, wants to believe that they have a purpose. They want to be reassured that there's a reason for life itself and that they, personally, have a unique life purpose. Does life need a purpose? Perhaps not. Do people feel more fulfilled when they believe they have a purpose? Mostly. Are they more focused, motivated, and happy when they are aligned with their Soul Purpose? Absolutely, and that's what I intend to show you through this book.

By the way, David is a real person. And his purpose is not just about the work he does to make money—something in music rather than tax consulting—it is about all of the areas he asked about. In other words, your relationships, your financial well-being, health, and general emotional state are all part of your true purpose, not just your job.

Unfortunately, like David on his first foray into his psyche, too many people wait until they're sure they aren't on their path before they learn the skills to navigate. They learn clearly what they don't want, and are confused about how they got there.

This book is for David and all of the other men and women who know there must be more to life. Somewhere inside, their soul is speaking to them and encouraging them to find and do their purpose. My purpose in writing this book is to help you let go of whatever has led you away from your true purpose—and to lead you through the steps to get back on track.

What Is Soul Purpose?

Throughout the book I will be using the term *Soul Purpose* to mean the life path that would best align you with your highest possibility for happiness, fulfilment, and joy. It is the same thing as your life purpose, your life's work, or your perfect vocation. However, in my definition, Soul Purpose encompasses all aspects of your life. It includes your relationships, your health, your financial comfort and what you contribute through paid or volunteer work. When you ask "Why am I here?" and you look beyond what you do for a living, the answer is "to create and fulfil your Soul Purpose."

We All Have One

I believe that we all have a unique, passionate, uplifting purpose that's permanently imprinted in our very cells. Unfortunately, most of us are looking for a purpose that relates to what our ego hopes we are here to do. We look around at what seems to drive other people and try to fit ourselves into a form that will bring one or more of the magic five: fame, fortune, power, love, or approval.

It Comes From The Inside

Soul Purpose is a co-creative process involving all aspects of you and your life. For your life path to be fulfilling, passionate and joyous it requires a connection between you and your spirit, from the inside. It requires connection with your body, mind, heart, and soul, and a courageous willingness to express on the outside what is true for you on the inside. Unfortunately, this requires a rewiring of the way many people are taught to navigate their lives.

Most of us look outside ourselves to decide who and what to be. We learn to check with our peers to make sure we're wearing the *right* clothes. We read the magazines or go on the Net to choose a car. We pick a job based on what pays well and is in demand. We check the best-seller lists for what to read, what music to listen to, and which movies to watch.

I'm not saying that checking with others is unwise. It's just that this is typically, for many people, the only way they know how to operate. It becomes their natural way of choosing everything they do and think and feel. Few of us are taught to check inside first, or, at the very least, to check inside after we have explored the ideas of others. To create and then follow your Soul Purpose requires checking in with *yourself* first and last.

The Skills of Soul Purpose

This first skill of Soul Purpose, the skill to check in with yourself and to make decisions from the inside, requires time and patience to develop. It requires skill in identifying what your body is feeling, physically and emotionally, awareness of your thoughts, and conscious discernment about whether or not you are connected to your soul or Higher Self.

Most people whom I have met and worked with have developed little of this skill. It is not required on most job descriptions. And yet, it is precisely these skills that will bring you the capacity to create and manifest a life of joyous fulfilment, purpose, and soulful living. In chapters 5 and 6, I will outline the skills that will help you develop the natural abilities required to manifest a life on purpose.

> *It's not a doing thing —it's a being thing.*

Most people usually relate purpose to some form of work, paid or unpaid. They focus on what they are *doing* or what they think they would enjoy *doing*. This is limited thinking. When you're looking for your purpose, look in all areas of your life, at all levels, and think about what you want to be *being*.

Your Soul Purpose is not a *doing* thing; it's a *being* thing. It's not about *doing* someone's taxes as an accountant. It's not about building houses as a carpenter. It's not about sitting at a keyboard as a writer. It *is* about how you feel, what you're experiencing, how you're being, on all levels, in a particular moment, while you're doing your life's work. It *is* about *being* happy, connected, fulfilled, abundant, and in service.

Do We Have Choice?

Probably the most frequently asked question about Soul Purpose is this: "Is it predefined or do we get to choose?" I think that the answer is *yes* to both, depending on the level from which you answer. If you answer from the perspective that we are all one, i.e., that we and The Creator are all one being then the answer is "Yes, Soul Purpose is predefined. All of us share the purpose of assisting God in experiencing him/herself in all of the possible forms we create on the earth plane." And, if you answer from the perspective that each of us is an individuated soul, the answer is "Yes, we get to choose our Soul Purpose. Meaning, we have free will to decide *who* we will create ourselves to be, in order to fulfil that higher purpose of being a part of God. This is why life can seem so paradoxical—because it is!

So, stop wondering about *destiny* and decide right now, right here while you're holding this book that *you get to choose who you want to be*. As Neale Donald Walsch says so boldly in his *Conversations with God*,[2] create yourself "in the next grandest version of the greatest vision ever you held about who you are." Use your free will to choose the essence of who you want to express, and allow the form of that essence to be created out of your willing it so.

We do have choice. There is no destiny other than the one we choose together. We have all chosen to express an aspect of God. Which aspect, we have choice about. The universe decides how it will manifest in physical form.

What Drives Most People's Life Work?

Many people's actions are primarily ego-driven because that is how they are influenced to behave. However, I believe that fundamentally, at a core level, we are driven by our soul. The better we are able to harness the power of both the ego and the soul, and act on the inspiration of both, the closer we will be to our true purpose.

When we allow the ego to drive our purpose, without the expanded view of our soul, we will probably stray from our ideal path. How do we start off on the wrong foot in the first place? Here are two examples. These are representative of some of the basic events that, followed by years of reinforcing experiences, shape our initial orientation toward Soul Purpose.

The first event is when your own sense of what's right for you is superseded by the will of someone else. Unfortunately, this is a common experience in most people's infancy and childhood. For example, you're 12 months old and crawling on the living room floor. You feel as if it's time to begin exploring further afield. You wander over to the stairs and begin to climb, exercising your inner explorer. Mom or dad sees you at the edge of the staircase and rushes over to save you from perceived danger. You are scolded for wandering somewhere that is *dangerous* in someone else's view. In that moment you learn that your own inner sensing is not as good as someone else's. That *someone else* is usually a parent, yet it may be a sibling or peer.

Now, I'm not saying that we should allow children to wander into danger. I am saying that we adults teach children, in most cases, that our idea of what is good, safe, acceptable, and valuable, is more valid than their own inner sensing. We often stop infants from exploring and testing their own inner sensing long before they are in any real danger. So, *the first event that shapes our orientation toward Soul Purpose is often doubt of our own inner sensing.*

The second event is when you decide what you will allow to motivate your actions. This is the beginning of your value system. This is when you begin to seek fame, fortune, power, love or approval. I call these the *magic five*. You experience one or more of these directly and decide, "That was nice—I want more," or you experience someone else seeking these and decide, "I should want that. It seems like that's what life is about." *The second event that shapes our orientation to our life purpose is when we decide what we want to seek in order to feel satisfied.*

Of course, I'm simplifying and generalizing a lot here. The two basic events I've described that orient us around Soul Purpose are unique in their specific details for everyone. Yet, in some way or another, unless you're an ascended master or fully evolved being, we all carry some aspect of these two basic issues in our own special way. Please note: if you are a fully evolved being, please skip ahead to the end of the book—you probably know all this stuff already.

Let's get specific. When Paul was one year old he decided to pick up his bowl of cereal and dump it on his head. It felt nice running down his face and made a nice puddle on the tray of the highchair for playing with his spoon. His inner feelings said, "Yes, this is a good thing. I want to do this again." Then his father caught him tipping the bowl over his head and smacked his hand. He thinks, "Maybe dumping the bowl is not a good idea because I get hurt afterwards." He decides that his own experience means less than what his father says is the right thing to do. He stops tipping the bowl and thinks twice before taking exploratory risks in the future. Step one in Paul's orientation towards his purpose is that he sets aside his inner sensing about exploring and leans towards waiting to see what the authority figure thinks first.

A few days later Paul is playing in the living room and his older brother Tim comes in from playing baseball at school. His father runs over and hugs Tim and says, "I'm so proud of you for being such a great athlete son!" Paul decides, "Aha, the way to my father's heart is through sports. I'll do that instead of exploring my physical senses with my cereal. A much safer option." And, presto, Paul has made his first decision in step two of shaping his orientation towards his purpose. He has learned to value pleasing someone else rather than himself, and to value athletic prowess.

At the ripe young age of one, Paul is limited in choosing a life purpose that satisfies his own inner urgings and his own sense of pleasure. This is just one story of one little boy. Each of us has our own stories, on many levels, that lead us off our own true path. In chapter 4, I will explore in greater detail the many kinds of issues that keep people from being happy and fulfilled in their purpose, as well as how to heal those issues.

How Do You Know It's Your Purpose?

You will know that you're doing your purpose if the following elements are true. You will feel fulfilled, connected to yourself and what you do, and connected to your soul. You will have a moment where you experience joy and a sense of flow in what you are doing. Many things around you will seem to support you in doing your purpose. The Universe will provide you with opportunities to heal whatever is in the way of doing your purpose and will give you life experiences to learn the necessary awareness and skills.

A Note About Developing Talents

You may be wondering whether our natural talents are a good indicator of our purpose. Yes, they are. All of us came into this life with unique gifts and talents tailored specifically to suit our Soul Purpose. The gifts are just there—nice little parcels of natural ability carried forward from past lives, genetic inheritance or through blessings from God. The gifts are indicators of purpose only when they are used with love. Whenever you give yourself permission to do what you love to do, you are closer to your soul and in touch with the natural creative energies available to help you.

The dark side of natural talents is that they can be used to beat up others or ourselves. If you are really good at something you may beat others up for not being so good. You may also beat yourself up when you do not perform at a high level. Gifts can be a blessing or a burden to you or to others, depending on how you hold them in the world. By valuing your own gifts, and supporting others in developing theirs, you will naturally heal the issues that take you and others away from your Soul Purpose.

How Can Traditional Career Planning Evolve?

I have studied career development for almost two decades. I've taught all of the traditional skills in job search, resume writing, and career planning. None of the traditional theories help people to identify what makes them happy and fulfilled in their work on all levels: physically, emotionally, mentally, and spiritually. I believe the things that stir your feelings of happiness and fulfilment are guiding you to your purpose. In other words, if it feels really good, on all levels, it is what you are meant to be doing. We are here to enjoy.

I decided to abandon all the traditional thinking and I interviewed hundreds of people to discover and analyze life purpose. What I found was that everyone could talk about particular moments of happiness and what they were feeling and being at the time. Again, what elicits happiness is your purpose. The first place to look to understand your purpose is the moments in your life when you feel the most joy, satisfaction, or fulfilment.

Through identifying the components of those moments of joy (where they were, who they were with, how they were interacting with people and things in the environment, what they were doing and how they were being) people were able to gather clues about the source of their happiness. This, in turn, led them to understand their purpose or what they felt compelled to do in the world. I call this description of your purpose the "*Energetic-of-Soul Purpose.*"

I have used the phrase *Energetic-of-Soul Purpose* because I want to totally change the way you see life purpose. I wanted to find a phrase that conveys to you that your life purpose is not just something you do. It is not just your job in the world and it is not just an action that you take. It is an experience that you create with your soul, in order to raise yourself and the world towards more happiness. It is your creation, powered by the energy of your soul.

Your Soul Purpose is your contribution to yourself and the world. It provides energy for others, and it attracts energy to you. Hence, I have used *energetic* to describe the moment when you are doing your Soul Purpose. So, for you, your *Energetic-of-Soul Purpose* will describe your physical, emotional, mental, and spiritual experience when you are *doing* your Soul Purpose.

You get to choose your purpose and create it in your life. And the pathway to identifying your purpose is through exploring what causes you to feel happy, fulfilled and self-actualized. Your

Energetic-of-Soul Purpose describes the physical, emotional, mental, and spiritual levels of what you are being and doing when you feel happy and fulfilled.

I will start by first helping you to analyze and describe your *Energetic-of-Soul Purpose*. This is stage one. Then, later in the book, you will see how to use the *energetic* to attract experiences where you get to do your Soul Purpose. I call this *magnetizing* your Soul Purpose. This is stage two and it will be described in detail in chapter 6.

Although I have said already that Soul Purpose is not just about what you do for a living, your job is a good place to begin to explore your *energetic*. This is because it is often easier for you to see what you contribute in the workplace than it is to see what you contribute in close personal relationships or in your family. Because someone is paying you, it is easier to focus on what you're giving and receiving on a practical level.

Let's start with an example and then break it down so you understand what to look for and what the *Energetic-of-Soul Purpose* means. If you were an accountant, here's a description of your *energetic* and the type of job you may fit, followed by a traditional job description:

The perfect *energetic* for Joe Accountant's Soul Purpose:

- Using his creative visioning and problem-solving abilities;
- Working with people of like-mind;
- Streamlining financial planning and administration functions;
- Working in the automotive, technological, and printing industries;
- Motivating, inspiring, and brainstorming with others;
- Finding balance by being in nature and having private time to think and integrate group experiences.

This would translate into a job that Joe may fit, as follows:

Joe is working in a supportive company where his boss and co-workers care about his success and the satisfaction of their customers. He works with a team of financial specialists to guide the financial planning and administration of a mid-sized automotive company. He feels fulfilled when he develops creative ideas for building financial stability. He is most happy leading his team and encouraging their creative ideas. He uses his gifts in motivating as well as his natural talent with finances. He is also inspired when working with management to guide the future vision. He loves his place of work, with a comfortable, private office and a park nearby.

Here is a traditional job description for an accountant:

Responsible for the financial planning and accounting of a mid-sized automotive company. Manages five staff, including an assistant financial analyst, two bookkeepers, a clerk and a secretary. Duties include preparation of financial statements, payroll, accounts payable and receivable, and preparation of financial planning statements for *vision* meetings of the executive team.

Which of the above descriptions sounds more appealing? The first, of course. You may be saying to yourself, "The first one sounds better, but that job would be harder to find." True, the kind of environment that would welcome and support the *energetic* may be rare. However, by analyzing and describing the moment that makes you happy, and the components of that moment, you are many times more likely to be able to manifest a job where you can recreate that moment and have it as often as possible.

Let's break down Joe's *energetic* to help you understand what to look for in your own *energetic*. Joe would review past jobs and life experiences looking for moments of feeling happy, fulfilled, connected, in the *flow*, and in service to himself and others. He focuses on his whole life, not just paid work, looking for moments of joy, and feeling in the flow. He would analyze each experience on four levels: physical, emotional, mental, and spiritual.

Joe realized that support from his boss and co-workers was a key to his happiness, and a part of the emotional environment that supports him in doing his purpose. One of the physical environments that works best for him is the automotive industry, in a mid-to-large size company. He loves cars and is interested in mechanics. He is happiest in a location where he has a comfortable office and someplace nearby to walk in nature at lunch time.

The moment that makes him happiest has to do with motivating others to be creative or in being creative and visionary himself. This is part of his mental environment where his intellect and imagination are appreciated and nurtured. He realizes he also does this with his family and friends, encouraging others to connect to their creativity. Finally, his spiritual environment is addressed by working with people who care about him and the products and services they provide.

This first step helps us recognize that we are multi-dimensional beings and we experience life on four primary levels. Therefore, whatever makes us happy needs to address those four levels. Next, let's take a closer look at the steps so you can see how your *energetic* will work for you.

TWO

Identifying Your

"Energetic-of-Soul Purpose"

THE way we typically manifest the next job has more to do with analyzing skills and technical experiences and selling those skills to an employer. Using the *energetic* technique you get clear on the kinds of experiences you want to be having daily and weekly. The traditional way of preparing you to get the next job focuses just on skills, abilities and practical experience. With the *energetic* process you track much more of your feelings: physically, emotionally, mentally, and spiritually. You remember your best moments and focus on what you were feeling, giving, and receiving.

The power of the *energetic* technique is in its use of our natural manifesting abilities. This technique uses your body, heart, mind and spirit in the same way that creative visualization works when you add the sensations of physical, emotional and spiritual feelings to the pictures in your mind.

And, before you can effectively use your body, heart, mind and spirit to manifest you must do the research to uncover those moments in your life you want to repeat and enhance. This is the first stage in identifying your *Energetic-of-Soul Purpose*.

It is important to take the time—as much as you need—to go through the steps one by one, tuning in to how you experienced each situation in the past. You may get some of the same information for more than one of the steps. That's OK because each step just takes you deeper into examining the information from the previous steps.

So how do *you* get started to find the *energetic* of your purpose—the first stage in understanding your life's work? Below are the steps that guide you through the personal research to identify your *Energetic-of-Soul Purpose*. Although the steps focus on your jobs, keep in mind that your life purpose encompasses every area of your life. As you find moments of happiness in your work you will notice that similar ways of being cause you to be happy in all other areas of your life.

The final step is to use the *energetic* to attract experiences in your life where you get to live the *energetic* as often as you like. In other words, the last step is to manifest your Soul Purpose. I call this *magnetizing* your Soul Purpose because it guides you in changing yourself from the inside so that you become *magnetic* to the people, places, and opportunities you will require to do your Soul Purpose. Chapter 6 will tell you how to do this successfully.

I will go through the steps three times, using a general example and then provide specific examples using two people. One of them is relatively happy in her work so her *Energetic-of-Soul Purpose* is more obvious. The second example is a person who has fewer moments of happiness, so he works a little harder to find his *energetic*. Keep in mind that the same steps apply even if you are not currently working for pay or have never received a paycheque. Instead of reviewing all your jobs you review all life experiences looking for moments of happiness.

Stage 1 (steps 1 to 9) guide you in describing your *Energetic-of-Soul Purpose*. You will recall that your *Energetic-of-Soul Purpose* is how you are feeling, and being, as well as what you are doing, when you are experiencing your Soul Purpose. The main focus of the first nine steps is to aid you in identifying moments in your life when you felt happy, fulfilled, or self-actualized. These are the moments when you were closest to your Soul Purpose.

Stage 2 (step 10) guides you in creating opportunities to do your Soul Purpose.

Stage 1: Describing your "Energetic-of-Soul Purpose"

Step 1: **Review all of your past jobs, paid and unpaid, and describe, in detail, the moments you loved the most**.

Focus your descriptions on what you were doing, who you were interacting with, and the results. For example, let's say you were a family lawyer and your favourite moment was counselling your clients. Describe the kinds of clients you enjoyed the most, which of your talents you used to assist them, and the difference that your advice created in their lives.

Note: if you cannot think of even one moment that you loved while working, expand the exercise to include your whole life. Pick several moments that you loved. Later in this chapter, I'll take you through an example with a man who had never experienced much joy while working. You'll see how he looks into other areas of his life, besides work, to find what brings him joy.

Step 2: **Analyze those moments of joy and describe them on all four levels: physical, emotional, mental, and spiritual**.

For example, like the lawyer, you may have experienced feeling physically relaxed as you reviewed your client's files while sitting comfortably in your office; feeling emotionally calm and centred as you analyzed the information, and energized and elated as you tuned in to specific ideas to help your clients resolve their problems; thinking (mental level) that your intuition was helping you to provide advice and deciding that you were pleased to be helping people; and feeling spiritually at peace with yourself, and connected to your clients and your own true purpose.

Step 3: **Relive, in your mind and body, one of the most powerful moments of joy, and capture the human dynamic**.

Ask yourself these questions: *Who was I interacting with? What were they seeking, asking, and doing? What was I doing in response?* Sometimes you are physically alone in your moment of joy. In that case, think of the person or people who benefited from your actions and ask the same questions as above in relationship to them.

For example, you're a web-site developer. Your moments of joy are mostly about creating some cool new twist on a site that you know will attract lots of *hits*. Usually it's just you and the computer when you experience that joy. Then you think about how the clients and the web surfers have responded to your creativity. They are seeking something new, innovative and attractive—something that will bring clients back to the site over and over again. In response you're taking the time to get to know the clients and what they want, interviewing web users and reading the marketing reviews to understand their needs. Then you're letting your mind and body take you into a creative space to capture something unique.

Step 4: **Capture, internally, *how* you do what you do**.

This may be challenging. Most people will respond by saying "I don't know how I do that!" This is a good sign. It means you are probably focusing on the right moments because it should seem so easy that you don't know how you do it. Focus anyway. Close your eyes. Sit still with your feet flat on the floor. Take yourself back to one of those moments. Trace what you did to get there. How did you feel about yourself in that moment? What were you connected to internally, externally?

For example, you're a trainer. Your moment of joy is when the participants in your training sessions have an *aha*—they finally *get* some new insight or creative idea. When you relive your moment, focusing on what you did to get there, you realize you were feeling confident about your material, connected to the energy of the group, and caring about the learning. You were connected to your own internal knowledge and experience, as well as connected to others.

Step 5: **Analyze, in minute detail, the environment which best supports your moments of joy**.

Were you inside or outside? In a group or alone? What kinds of people were you with? Describe the physical environment—furniture, building, location, as well as the emotional, mental and spiritual environment. If you can imagine an even better environment than you have ever experienced, describe that as your ideal.

For example, you're a customer service representative for a telecommunications company. Your moments of joy happen when you are working independently as part of a larger, supportive team. You realize that it is important for you to have the support of your team and to have other reps around you that you can coach and support. Your manager gives you a good balance between strong leadership and direction and autonomy. You have a comfortable office space with ergonomically designed furniture, windows, and beautiful pictures on the walls. You feel physically comfortable, mentally stimulated by the work and your co-workers, and emotionally supported and confident.

You stretch your imagination further and realize that it would be even more perfect if you felt good about the principles of your company—this would give you the spiritual sense of connection to your larger community. You make a note to seek ways to achieve this where you are or to consider moving to a different company in the future.

Step 6: **Define the service or exchange of energy that transpired**.

What did you give and receive? Was it an exchange of services, ideas or products? Track the exchange on all levels: physical, emotional, mental, and spiritual.

For example, if you are an auto technician you exchange your mechanical knowledge and repair skills for money. You may also receive emotional satisfaction from feeling that you served your client well. You feel mentally stimulated when a client arrives with an especially challenging problem. Spiritually you may experience a feeling of connection and flow when working on the car—as if you are sensing the perfect adjustments on the motor.

You also realize that there is a larger exchange that happens between you and your community. You sponsor several local baseball teams for kids. In return you feel proud of your contribution to kids' learning, and clients are attracted to your business when they see your company name on the back of the baseball sweaters.

Step 7: **Track the feedback that you got from others immediately, and later.**

How did others respond to what you did? Did they comment on the gifts you expressed in your *moment*, or the product or service that was created? What did they say about you, the experience, and the results?

For example, if you are a massage therapist, others may remark that they feel more relaxed or that stiff joints have more mobility. Over a longer period of time, clients may comment that they feel safe opening up to you and sharing their lives while receiving the massage. They may comment on your professional manner, kindness, or soothing energy.

Some feedback may be less immediate as in the work of a gardener. The results may show up much later, when flowers bloom and trees bear fruit.

Step 8: **Identify the Universal Energy you were expressing in your moments of joy?**

These are the *biggies* that most of us admire and aspire to express, such as love, joy, charity, peace, and harmony. For a complete list of possible Universal Energies (U.E.'s) see Appendix 1. There may be more than one that applies to you. Here's a clue: whatever you dislike and typically judge in other people, write it down and then think of the opposite. This will usually be a U.E. for you. For example, you have a hard time with messy, disorganized people. The opposite of messy is orderly. *Order* is one of your U.E.'s.

For example, you are a child caregiver in your own home daycare. When you relive the most joyful moments you realize that you were expressing your love for the children. Love is a Universal Energy that you put into all the things you care about.

It bothers you when people are inconsiderate or forget to acknowledge what they have received. You're always reminding the children to say *thank you*. You realize that *gratitude* is another one of your Universal Energies.

Step 9: **Clarify your intent in your moments of joy**.

It may take some backtracking to get to the original intent. This is the place that you were coming from, on all levels, as you were in your joy moment. To backtrack, ask yourself *What is my intent in doing this?* Whatever you get as an answer, ask *And so, why do I do that?* Keep backtracking until you feel you're at the core of your intent.

Let's say your moment is when you are teaching young children to sing in your daycare facility. When you think back to the reason you were teaching them you realize it is because you do care about the lives of others. You want to ensure that young people feel loved and fulfilled.

When you ask yourself *Why do I do that?* you realize that your intent at a deeper level is to create a world where people are more loving, expressive, and powerful. This reminds you of how you love to feel yourself. Your true intent is to share your happiness with others through having a loving impact on young people.

Stage 2: Magnetizing Your Soul Purpose

You have seen examples of answers to the questions in steps 1 – 9: Describing Your *Energetic-of-Soul Purpose*. The next stage guides you in creating opportunities to *do* your Soul Purpose.

Step 10: **Use your *energetic* to magnetize situations where you get to live it as often as possible**.

This is the second stage in the process of manifesting your Soul Purpose. You get to use your natural manifesting abilities through creative visualization with the addition of the emotional, mental, and spiritual components, to attract situations where you get to relive your *Energetic-of-Soul Purpose* over and over again. Step 10 will be covered in detail in chapter 6.

Let's see how all the steps would fit together for Samantha, who is 43. She is currently an assistant to the sales manager at a car dealership and is also mother to two young boys, as well as leader of the church choir.

Step 1: **Review all of your past jobs, paid and unpaid, and describe, in detail, the moments you loved the most**.

Samantha lists the moments she loved the most:

Assistant to Sales Manager at A-1 Car Dealership: Love interacting with the clients when they are excitedly choosing a car or coming in to pick up their new car after servicing. Feel happy when the manager asks me to organize a staff party or sales meeting. Enjoy being part of the larger team and interacting with all of the sales reps.

Assistant to Manager at Department Store: Most happy when organizing meetings for sales staff, researching marketing techniques for new promotions, and interacting with staff to solve problems. Love the people and the feeling of helping others to be successful.

Leader of Church Choir: Love to see the children interacting with the adults and developing their confidence. Feel energized when performing on weekends and special holidays. Feel good when parents come up to me and thank me for encouraging their child.

Mother of Two Boys Aged 7 and 9: Feel fulfilled when the boys demonstrate their citizenship by walking younger boys to school or helping to organize the school play. Love to help them learn by tutoring them in schoolwork or taking them to participate in community events.

Step 2: Analyze those moments of joy and describe them on all four levels: physical, emotional, mental, and spiritual.

Samantha examines the moments more deeply on all four levels. Physically, I feel energized and relaxed in all the moments I described. I like my office because it's comfortable—just like my home. Emotionally I'm happy and having fun at work, with my kids, and with the choir. I feel mentally stimulated in the sales environment and learn a lot about marketing. Spiritually, I love to help others feel good about themselves and I do that with my sales team, the choir members and my kids. I realize I do that with my family too.

Step 3: Relive, in your mind and body, one of the most powerful moments of joy, and capture the human dynamic.

Samantha picks a moment when the choir was invited to perform at a Christmas celebration for the local community. When she relives the experience she realizes that her heart felt open as she stood in front of the choir and felt their personal satisfaction in expressing their gifts.

She remembers sensing her connection to the adults and kids and feeling that she loved them as equals. The members of the choir were seeking to create a beautiful, harmonious sound and Samantha was leading them to love and connect to each other in their songs.

Step 4: **Capture, internally, *how* you do what you do.**

Samantha closed her eyes and took herself back to that Christmas celebration. She feels the exhilaration in her body and some butterflies in her stomach. As she scans her body she feels her heart open and connected to her own love of music.

She notices that she is holding a high image of all of the people in the choir and they respond to her high expectations by fulfilling them. On another level she is aware of the audience and wanting them to feel the music and enjoy the beauty. She loves the moments when they applaud and acknowledge the gifts of the choir. Most of all she realizes that she does what she does because of her love of music and people.

Step 5: **Analyze, in minute detail, the environment which best supports your moments of joy.**

At work and at home Samantha requires comfort and relaxation. She likes a balance between independent time alone and busy time with lots of people around. The colour and look of the furniture is important to her. She loves bright, vibrant, winter colours, like forest green, navy blue and black. Her office is welcoming, with many fun accents from various craft shows, as well as homemade floral decorations.

She enjoys people who are kind and considerate. Her favourite sales reps are always the ones with a good sense of humour who help others to succeed. Samantha realizes she has a difficult time with people who are negative.

Step 6: **Define the service or exchange of energy that transpired.**

Samantha has a more challenging time identifying this one. Although she is aware that she is helping the choir members, she is reluctant to take credit for the contribution she is making. I suggested that Samantha ask several other people to give her feedback on the contribution she makes.

After getting feedback from several friends, and with some coaching to allow herself to focus on what she offers, she concludes that it is her belief that other people are genuinely good and that everyone has something of value to offer others. She can see that she helps the sales reps and her manager to feel good about themselves. This also shows up with the kids in her choir. They shine even more when she's around. Samantha learns that she doesn't take in the true value of her contributions; others had to point this out to her.

Step 7: **Track the feedback that you got from others immediately, and later.**

Samantha thinks back to her last performance review at work. Her boss said she was a good team player, excellent at organizing staff events, and above the ordinary in meeting the needs of customers.

Again I suggested that Samantha check in with people who know her at work as well as personally. Sometimes you need to see yourself through someone else's eyes to see your true value.

They remind her of acknowledgment that she didn't notice at the time it was given. A co-worker on her team at work reminds her that she receives at least one thank-you card a week from customers who appreciated her outstanding service. One married couple even sent her flowers. One of Samantha's friends who helps out with the choir remembers several parents going up to her after the practices and hugging her and saying how much they appreciated Samantha's gifts, and her encouragement of their child to be expressive and disciplined.

Samantha takes in acknowledgment that she had forgotten. Through the minds and hearts of her friends and co-workers, she begins to open and receive the goodness that's all around her and sees her own gifts more clearly.

Step 8: **Identify the Universal Energies you were expressing in your moments of joy**.

It's getting easier for Samantha to see herself and to track her Universal Energies because she is getting help from people close to her. She feels that *beauty* and *love* are biggies for her. The beauty is manifested in the way she sees beauty in everyone around her. It's also in the music she creates through her choir.

Love threads through her whole life. She loves her family, friends, co-workers, boss, and children in the choir.

She loves herself enough to create beauty and comfort in her home and at work. It becomes clear to her that this is what she gives to others—the capacity to love themselves more.

Step 9: **Clarify your intent in your moments of joy**.

After all the soul-searching Samantha has done to answer the questions in the first eight steps, she feels close to knowing her true intent. She time travels back in her mind to her moment of joy. She feels herself there on stage with all of the kids around her and the audience listening intently. She feels her connection to the kids, herself, the audience.

What stands out the most is her joy in hearing the powerful voices and seeing the happiness on the kids' faces. She asks herself *Why do I do this?* In her mind she answers herself: *Because I love to feel people enjoying their own power. I love to be a part of something that helps others feel powerful!*

She sees that her intent is to love people enough for them to recover and express their personal power.

Step 10: **Use your *energetic* to magnetize situations where you get to live it as often as possible**.

Samantha will join us in Chapter 6 to magnetize her joyful moment.

You might be thinking that Samantha is almost too good to be true. She had an easy time identifying and describing her moments of joy because there are so many of them in all areas of her life. You might be wondering "What about me! I don't remember ever being happy at work or anywhere. And my family life, it's non-existent. I never see my partner or my kids because I'm working my buns off just to make ends meet. How will I ever find my *Energetic-of-Soul Purpose*?"

You can. It's there. We all have one. Don't despair.

It may take much work to uncover it. You may have fewer happy moments you can relate to your Soul Purpose. But they are there, inside of you. You may need lots of healing and learning in order to find and do your life purpose. And you can still create it, no matter where you're at now.

Here's another example of how the steps work. This time we'll look at William's *Energetic-of-Soul Purpose*. William has had few moments of joy. He doesn't associate work with pleasure. For him, work is something you do to earn an income. Pleasure is what you feel in your free time. William took a leap of faith in working through the steps to help him find his *energetic*.

William's most recent job was delivering pizzas part-time while he studied computer programming at night school. He is 36 years old and unmarried with no children. His job history includes executive assistant to a vice-president of financial management for a large advertising company.

Step 1: **Review all of your past jobs, paid and unpaid, and describe, in detail, the moments you loved the most.**

William lists the moments he loved the most:

Executive Assistant at XYZ Advertising: hated most of the job, especially the long hours, constant pressure, and the arrogance of the account executives. Some redeeming factors: working downtown with an exciting array of shops and fun nightlife, as well as the fairly decent pay, with benefits; enjoying the fun of mixing with some of the creative people in the design area; meeting interesting women.

Delivery Person for Vito's Pizza: Loved the autonomy of being out on the road and being my own boss. Felt respected by the owner and staff. Close to home. Poor pay but it got me through night school.

There wasn't much here to show William what he loved, so I asked about hobbies and things he did that were unpaid.

Hobbies: Love to hack around on my computer, especially checking out new graphics programs and games with exciting visuals. Belong to a computer club where we're building a new graphics enhancement feature for a well-known drawing program.

Enjoy walking in the woods, especially by water. Take my digital camera with me and shoot pictures of the trees, streams, and birds. Then I load the images into my computer and enhance them with special effects. I get a fun response from my friends when I pass them along in my e-mails.

Now that William has tuned in to some things that he enjoys in his free time we can see a small link back to his description of what he liked at the advertising company. He said, "Enjoying the fun of mixing with some of the creative people in the design area." He has an obvious attraction to creative design, which shows up in the people he likes to be with, his interest in computer graphics, and his love of photography.

This gives William a place to focus to get a handle on his *Energetic-of-Soul Purpose.*

Step 2: **Analyze those moments of joy and describe them on all four levels: physical, emotional, mental, and spiritual.**

William examines the moments more deeply on all four levels. He thinks back to a fun moment with the computer. He remembers staying up all night when he bought his first graphics program for creating his own cartoons. He takes himself back to that night to get in touch with what was going on inside. He felt expanded, as if a whole new world of possibilities had been opened up. He forgot about the time and felt totally absorbed in his first cartoon creation.

He remembers thinking, "The guys are going to crack up laughing when I send them this cartoon." He also shared that he felt free, with no one telling him what to do or how to create his cartoons. Emotionally he felt happy, relaxed, and confident.

Tracking the spiritual level was a big stretch for William. I coached him: "What did you feel connected to inside or outside? Where do you think the creative ideas were coming from? What part of you was feeling passionate about the task?"

He felt he was connected to a part of himself he remembers from childhood. He used to watch cartoons and marvel at how real the characters looked. He imagined creating his own stories with cool characters that could take over the world. He felt the ideas came from his heart. His heart and mind were connected and feeling passionate about creating something which others could laugh at and enjoy.

Step 3: **Relive, in your mind and body, one of the most powerful moments of joy, and capture the human dynamic**.

William picks a moment from that all-nighter when he drew this powerful Darth Vader looking character that he called *The Blue Force*. He remembers thinking about his best friend, Tom, and imagining him opening the e-mail file and being blown away by *The Blue Force*. He was also time travelling into the future and fantasizing about creating a computer game with this character as the central figure in a war of the worlds.

As William relived his moment, and got in touch with his joy about how others would react, he realized how much he wants positive feedback from his friends. He would like to get feedback from others too—in a big, public way—developing games for the worldwide market.

Step 4: **Capture, internally, *how* you do what you do**.

William closed his eyes and took himself back to that time at his computer. He thought about what he did to get into that place of creativity. He recalls feeling free and remembers how he felt inspired by the sample graphics in the instruction booklet for the graphics program. He let his mind go into total, uninhibited, creative fun—just like he was a child again. He felt like time stood still and everything around him stopped. His focus was on the creative elements of the program and how his friends would enjoy what he had brought to life.

He captures the essential elements of how he does what he did: uninterrupted time by himself, having the tools (graphics program) to work with to create, inspiration from what others have created, freedom to allow his mind to enter an altered state of consciousness, and passion about the anticipated response from others.

Step 5: **Analyze, in minute detail, the environment which best supports your moments of joy**.

At work and at home William requires a healthy balance between working alone and time to mix with other creative minds. He doesn't require fancy furniture or up-to-date office space; however, he wants the latest computer programs and fancy peripherals. He is attracted to people about his own age who are also into graphics, photography, and anything digital. His one essential criterion is autonomy—the freedom to design, create, and operate under his own supervision.

Step 6: **Define the service or exchange of energy that transpired**.

This is a new concept for William. He thought he was in service to himself when he created his cartoon characters. He asks himself, "What did I give and receive?" He realizes he gave his creative energies, knowledge of computer graphics, and zany sense of humour. In return he got positive feedback from his buddies. In the future the exchange will include being paid to design these characters (if things go the way he wants).

He tracks the exchange on all levels: physically, he produces a cartoon and receives praise and excitement; emotionally, he feels happy, confident, excited and tickled by his own humour; mentally, he thinks he is good at what he does and is hopeful someone will recognize and pay for his talent; spiritually, he feels *in the flow* and connected to his passion.

Step 7: **Track the feedback that you got from others immediately, and later**.

William thinks back to several times when he sent out an e-mail to friends with an attachment of his cartoon. Right away he got three messages back with lots of enthusiasm: "Great work! You'll be the next great movie animator. *The Blue Force* is a riot, William—let's see more of him in action." He knows he's good because all his friends come to him when they're having difficulties with some new program or a graphics idea. At work his peers ask him for computer help all the time. In his computer group he's known as *The Whiz* for his fast, brilliant ideas and creativity.

Step 8: **Identify the Universal Energies you were expressing in your moments of joy**.

William scans the list and settles on *joy*. The cartoons and graphics are full of fun and humour. He realizes joy is a big part of his life. He always wants to make people laugh and enjoy themselves. That is why he has a challenging time with some of the overly serious folks with whom he works.

Step 9: **Clarify your intent in your moments of joy**.

After all the soul-searching William has done to go through the steps, he sees his true intent more clearly. And, he begins to see some patterns that have kept him from doing what he loves for a living. His intent is to bring joy to others through crafting bold, humourous characters that challenge the status quo.

He sees that he has some fears of being rejected by others who may not understand or accept his brand of humour. He also realizes that he rebels against authority, fearing that someone will take away his precious autonomy.

Notice what happened to William as he went through the steps. He realized there was not much joy in what he was currently doing to earn an income. He got a chance to relive some moments of joy and identify the essential elements of those moments. He got to see and think about the factors that have limited him from doing what he loves. In other words, he got to reflect on the thoughts and feelings that have limited him.

We'll meet up with William again in chapter 4 when I address the healing that's possible to remove these barriers.

Now, pause and make a commitment to yourself to answer the nine questions for identifying and grounding your *Energetic-of-Soul Purpose*, provided on pages 42 – 45. Do it right now or go directly to your calendar and set aside two, one-hour slots for answering the questions. Ask for the courage to know who you are and what you're here to experience. Write down your nine answers and then summarize them into a full **description of your** *energetic*. In chapter 6 we'll be using the description to powerfully manifest opportunities for you to do your Soul Purpose.

Step 1: Review all of your past jobs, paid and unpaid, and describe, in detail, the moments you loved the most.

_____
_____
_____
_____
_____
_____
_____
_____

Step 2: Analyze those moments of joy and describe them on all four levels: physical, emotional, mental, and spiritual.

_____
_____
_____
_____
_____
_____
_____
_____

Step 3: Relive, in your mind and body, one of the most powerful moments of joy, and capture the human dynamic.

_____
_____
_____
_____

_____

_____

_____

_____

Step 4: **Capture, internally, *how* you do what you do.**

_____

_____

_____

_____

_____

_____

_____

Step 5: **Analyze, in minute detail, the environment which best supports your moments of joy.**

_____

_____

_____

_____

_____

_____

_____

Step 6: **Define the service or exchange of energy that transpired.**

_____

_____

_____

_____

●
_____

Step 7: Track the feedback that you got from others immediately, and later.

_____

_____

_____

_____

_____

_____

_____

Step 8: Identify the Universal Energies you were expressing in your moments of joy.

_____

_____

_____

_____

_____

_____

Step 9: Clarify your intent in your moments of joy.

_____

_____

_____

_____

_____

_____

_____

Summary Description of your *Energetic-of-Soul Purpose*:

_____

_____

_____

_____

_____

_____

_____

_____

Here's the cool part: by going through steps 1 – 9 you'll clearly identify what helps you be happy and some of the things that are in the way of you doing your purpose. In other words, you'll see exactly why you aren't there already. And—this is even more cool—you'll be able to use the information from the steps, as well as the guidance in chapter 4, to remove what has been in the way. Then, using chapter 6, you can get right to magnetizing moments that match your *energetic*.

How You'll Feel When You're There

You may be asking, "Why bother doing all this work to describe my moment of joy? Is it going to make a difference?"

Yes. It is possible to identify the criteria for happiness, to remove whatever is in the way of doing it, and to do your Soul Purpose. It's worth the work.

Here's what you'll feel when you are there: fulfilled, motivated, and worthwhile. You'll feel connected to your soul—the part of you that knows the real you. You'll experience connection to yourself, your soul, and the world. It's worth finding and doing your Soul Purpose.

THREE

The Pathway

Why We Don't Do Our Purpose

THERE are many reasons why people get off the track of their true life purpose. In the first chapter, I described two types of moments in early childhood and the effects of those moments on how you navigate in the world. Both of these are universally applicable; they happen to many people. Two of the most common ways of being that take you away from your purpose are:

- doubting of your own inner sensing;
- looking outside of yourself to determine what to value in order to receive the magic five (fame, fortune, power, love, or approval).

Either of these ways of being may disconnect you from your own inner truth, and therefore away from your true path.

These Are Not Roadblocks—They're The Journey

Please keep in mind that the major life events that you have experienced are not *roadblocks* to doing your purpose—they are the *preparation*. The Universe only sends you as much energy to push you away from your path as you require to build the passion and gain the experiences that prepare you to do what you are here to do.

This may sound like a pat, New-Age explanation for the traumas and hardships along the way, so let me get specific and practical.

Your Greatest Challenges Prepare You

The *roadblocks* that we explored earlier—the life events that are really the journey—are the soul's way of preparing us to do our Soul Purpose.

Cary had a mother who died of cancer relatively early in life. Her mother didn't take care of herself. She gave all of her energy to her husband and children. On her deathbed she expressed her unhappiness with the way she allowed her life to unfold. Cary picked up the same orientation to life. She ended a failed marriage where she felt undernurtured and found herself with two teenage kids whose demands sapped her of her life-force energy.

Cary learned, by default, that she was the only one who could care for her. After years of waiting for someone to come along and love her, she realized she had to start with loving herself. Cary's Soul Purpose is to help women stay connected to themselves and their spirit during and after pregnancy and birth. Her journey prepared her by showing her the dramatic effects of disconnection to self that many women experience, including her mother and herself.

Earth is the planet of polarity: light and dark, evil and goodness, male and female, tragedy and joy. All of these polarities cause us to choose. Sometimes we learn what we want by experiencing what we don't want. Cary learned by watching her mother's response to death. She had the opportunity to choose: "Do I want to repeat my mother's life or choose a life of nurturing and fulfilment?" We will pick up Cary's story again in a few pages and let you know where her question led.

Pause, right this minute, and ask yourself, "Whose life have I witnessed that has shown me what I don't want?" Whatever you find when you ask that question is another clue to your purpose. Knowing what you don't want leads you to clarity about what you do want.

In many ways this planet is designed to cause us to evaluate things moment to moment. Everything seems to have a positive or negative aspect. In actual fact what appears to be positive has aspects of what appears to be negative, and vice versa. This is why it is important to notice the places on your path that feel *wrong* and to value them, rather than judge them. All moments, potentially, will lead you to your Soul Purpose.

The book *Friendship with God*,[3] by Neale Donald Walsch, explains polarity with eloquence:

God: *There is nothing in the Universe that is separate from anything else. Hot and cold are, therefore, the same thing in varying degrees. So, too, are sadness and joy.*

Neale: "What a terrific insight! I never thought of it that way. Sadness and joy are just two names. They are words we have used to describe different levels of the same energy."

It's Not A Straight Line

We often learn *what is so* by experiencing *what is not so,* which causes a lot of detours on our pathway to joy. This is upsetting to many people who think that they should arrive at their chosen destination via the most direct route. Your path to being in a state of profound joy, having heaven on Earth, and being on purpose will not be a straight line.

If you're at point A and your wildest dream is to be at point B, then that's probably the right thing to be asking for. If you desire to be at point B, your soul, at some level, is moving you towards it through that desire. However, in order to prepare you with the healings, learnings, and knowings that will allow you to be able to attract point B, you will have to go through some experiences that feel like detours. Otherwise you'd already be there.

There are good reasons why people are not doing their purpose. Most of these relate to ways of thinking, feeling, and being that require healing.

When you are at A and you ask the Universe to take you to B, you will definitely go there. However, the pathway will not look like the straight line below.

A   B

Most likely, it will look like this:

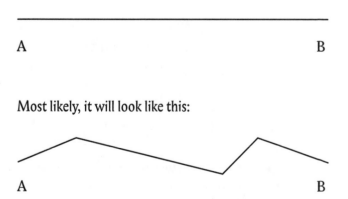

A   B

Let's say you're George, a carpenter, and your wildest dream is to race cars. You see racing cars as a sexy, macho kind of occupation for confident, cool dudes. Your current self-image is pretty poor. As a carpenter you feel pushed around by arrogant foremen. Your father dominated you and told you that you were *nothing*.

You pray and meditate, asking God to help you to be a race-car driver and then you follow your inner guidance system, acting on the messages that come to you internally. *Shazam*! Within three months you land a new job as a carpenter where you hate the foreman more than any before him. At this point you may be wondering, "Does this praying, affirmation, faith crap really work at all? I asked to race cars and feel confident, and here I am still sawing wood and taking lip from some jerk." Don't despair. Yes, prayer, affirmation, faith, and connection to Soul Purpose does work; however, your soul will take you through the paces first, so that when you end up at point B you're ready to receive it.

Here's how this applies to George. He's had low self-esteem all his life due to his response to his father's constant belittling and abusive put-downs. He is unprepared for the tough competition of men who face danger every day on the racetrack.

George is asking his Soul to help him feel more confident. So, what better way to heal his childhood than to have to face an abusive, belittling foreman every day? This gives George the opportunity to recapitulate his childhood and choose a new response. Rather than accepting the abuse and taking it personally he takes back his personal power one day by standing up to the foreman in front of the whole construction crew. The crew backs him up 100%. George feels great and decides that he is an OK man. His self-esteem grows and he feels safe enough to approach a car-racing school to take some lessons. What appeared to be a detour turns out to be just what George required to prepare to be at point B.

When You Ask, You Always Receive

Never doubt that your spirit is listening to and responding to your every request. Whatever comes back to you is a reflection of exactly what will assist you to achieve your highest purpose. It may not be what your ego asked for on the material plane; however, it is exactly what will help you the most to evolve, learn, heal, and grow towards your Soul Purpose. And, eventually, your material desires will be fulfilled as long as they are in your highest interests.

Sometimes We Only See The Next Inch

Many people ask me why they have never had a clear vision of what they should be doing in their lives. Vision needs a new marketing manager. First of all, vision requires connection to yourself: your body, mind, heart, and spirit. Most people have trouble keeping any one of these connections at any one time. To help you with these connections I've created a meditation to ground you and help you align with your soul. See Appendix 2.

Secondly, visions often come in several pieces, over a period of time, and arrive exactly when you need to receive and act on them. When you *catch the edge* of your vision you will either see it as attractive or not, depending on how much healing is needed. In some cases, if God were to show you exactly what you were here for and give you a vision of yourself doing it, you would self-combust, wither, and melt into oblivion.

Let's say you're destined to be the Pope. At age 10 God shows you a vision of yourself in robes and thousands of people worshipping you. You'd probably hide for a very long time and do as much as possible to deter yourself from achieving that vision. Or, let's say you're a little girl playing hopscotch at recess. Suddenly your head fills with a vision of millions of people watching you on TV as you swim the 100-meter race in the Olympics. It may or may not inspire you.

One more example: You are twenty years old and playing a computer game. Suddenly you see a vision of yourself at age forty, with three kids, and a wife. That looks good; you're excited. Then, you see more of the vision and notice that you have a mortgage, and aging parents.

You feel the weight of responsibility more than the joy of your accomplishments. You are also feeling some of your issues that require healing. You are feeling your Soul Purpose as a burden rather than a gift. You may turn back and be fearful of falling in love and marrying. You may not realize that the vision is just reflecting back to you the healing that is in the way of being totally happy doing your purpose.

Your soul only shows you what's in your highest interests in achieving the vision. If you do see a vision that feels heavy, trust that you are being shown exactly what you require. Rather than backing away in fear, bring the heaviness into the light and examine it. Perhaps there is a way to shift your thoughts and feelings so that *burdens* become gifts.

Usually your vision will come to you in smaller pieces and you'll often see the next inch along the path, not necessarily the next mile or the final result. It will come through your emotions as desire, motivation, interest, or passion. You'll feel drawn to a particular situation, person, place, or way of being. Follow that energy, each inch of the way, and eventually the path will fill in and become more recognizable. Because your soul is guiding the process, it may not make sense to you if you try to figure out the greater plan along the way.

Conversely, sometimes your soul will give you a glimpse of your higher purpose through admiration of the work of someone else. You may get a sense of passion about being like someone else or see yourself at point B in the future. Many people have these kinds of prophetic visions and discard them as arrogant, wishful thinking. Don't ignore those moments of dreaming of yourself as your highest self. As you are ready, your soul will give you those flashes to pique your interest and show you your potential. You wouldn't have the thoughts if it were not in some way possible.

Cary just lost her job. While at home in the void of unemployment she allowed herself to dream big. You'll recall in Cary's story that she and her mother had felt uncared-for. Cary decided she wanted to care for herself and help other women care for themselves. The first thing she thought about was helping women to have children in a more spiritual way. Until she did some research she didn't even know that there was a term for this work: spiritual midwifery. She couldn't see a way to do it with her current skills and abilities, yet she felt drawn to this work.

As in the stories above, she didn't end up at point B (spiritual midwifery) instantly. Her path led her first to working in a large telecommunications company, developing her ability to coach young people to own their gifts and connect to their higher abilities. Cary kept feeling pulled to the work of a spiritual midwife and looked for ways to build her confidence and coaching abilities, earning an income with the skills she had already developed in the workplace. She realized that coaching people in client service held many elements of helping people to connect to themselves—this is a skill she would require to be a spiritual midwife. By seeing the perfection in the detour on the path to point B, Cary was able to keep herself motivated and trusting that she was on her right path.

FOUR

Healing To Achieve

Your Soul Purpose

I N this chapter, I will outline several of the classic life experiences that may seem to have diverted you from doing your purpose. Then I will outline how healing can get you back on track. I call these experiences *founding moments*, which can be happy, higher-vibrational events, or unhappy, traumatic events.

Although the traumas seem to be in the way of our purpose, on another level, they are the wounds that give us the very experiences we require to be fully prepared to do our purpose. These are the issues that we seem to spend most of our lives healing. And, through the healing, we develop our capacity to fulfil our purpose.

Some of these life experiences pull us away from our true nature. They send us off on a journey from which many never return. I want to go slowly and carefully in this chapter, and give you a chance to find yourself in some of the stories, because I know it is possible for you to heal and to be doing your Soul Purpose. By examining the reasons why you are not doing your life's purpose you will be enabled to heal yourself, change, and get back on track.

Most of the experiences that have pulled you off your ideal path may seem small and insignificant upon close examination. You may ask, "If something that small could take me away from my life's purpose, how do any of us survive life and stay on track to complete our purpose?" This is a good question because it leads you to further recognize that the apparent *detours* are really part of the path.

In other words, it's not as if we come down to Earth to do our purpose and then the traumas and moments of suffering and separation get in the way. We choose those founding moments—the small ones and the large—specifically to attract the healing that will prepare us physically, mentally, emotionally and spiritually to do our Soul Purpose.

I don't mean we consciously pause and choose the moments of pain and suffering. We don't decide one day, "I think I'll get run down by a car so I can learn about suffering." When I say, "We choose those founding moments," I mean our Higher Self chooses—before we get here and while we're down here. It's not a present moment, conscious-thought kind of choosing.

Our Higher Self is the part of us that knows all of our past lives and future visions. It is loving and compassionate. It is our intuition, our inner voice, our soul, our connection to God, and our link to all of our past and future history. It only gives us as much energy to push us away from our purpose as we require to heal, and to learn what is necessary to get back on track and do it.

The Experiencing and Healing Cycle

Our lives are designed to flow through cycles of experiencing and healing. Within these cycles are moments of joy, sadness, pain, pleasure, fear, love, separation, and connection. Some moments cause us to expand and open, others cause us to contract and close. We experience life on four basic levels: physical, emotional, mental, and spiritual. Every moment is holographic: each part contains the whole experience. Regardless of what we are consciously aware of moment to moment, we take in every experience, and wire it in our cells, on all four levels.

Every experience, from the moment of conception onward, shapes us on those four levels. What we feel physically and emotionally, what we think mentally, and what we feel and believe spiritually, are shaped by our experiences.

What most people are unaware of consciously is the other half of the cycle, where we have opportunities to take those holograms and change them. This is healing. It can happen through life, as our Higher Selves take us naturally towards experiences that allow us to take limiting founding moments and make them unlimiting. Or, it can happen proactively, with the assistance of a facilitator, a healer.

Healing will not *take*, or undo the founding moment, unless the healing also happens on all four levels. This is an important distinction. Stop and think about the implications. This is why healing and therapy are not the same. This is why some forms of therapy appear to work and others do not, because the therapist may or may not be operating on all four levels. This is also true of some healers, by the way. They wonder why they get results sometimes and sometimes not. The difference is in whether the healing takes place on all four levels.

Let's examine this more deeply and tie it back to what you can do to release your limitations in doing your Soul Purpose.

Founding Moments

A *founding moment* is when a major change or trauma happens. It can be a happy, joyous moment or one filled with pain. You respond, on all levels, and your body, heart, mind and soul sort and evaluate the experience. You make major life decisions about yourself, others, the world, or spirit (usually God). These decisions, and the associated emotional energies, are literally wired into your cells; and they affect every other moment in your life—until and unless you heal them.

Most of us have our *founding moments* between the ages of zero and six years old, that is, from the time of conception to age six. You may be saying, "Wait a minute, how can we make decisions and feel things emotionally, physically and spiritually at the time of conception, or in the womb?" We do. We experience a lot and make a lot of decisions about ourselves, others, life, and God, that lay a powerful, formative foundation for the rest of our lives.

The founding moments get stored in our bodies and minds and become part of the context for how we perceive other experiences. This is what is known as cellular memory and it is worth repeating that it is holographic. In other words, every part of the memory, on every level, holds all of the other parts. For example, if something brings up the emotional part of the memory, the other parts, on the physical, mental, and spiritual levels, will surface also. Any aspect of the memory, on any one of the four basic levels, will bring up all other aspects of the memory.

The link between these founding moments and some of their effects on our health have been verified scientifically. In *Molecules of Emotion*, Candace Pert tells us "Just recently, researchers at the National Institutes of Health have found a link between depression and traumas experienced in early childhood. Studies have shown that abused, neglected, or otherwise unnurtured infants and children are more likely to be depressed as adults, and now we have a way to understand the link between the experience and the biology..."

"...When emotions are repressed, denied, not allowed to be whatever they may be, our network pathways get blocked, stopping the flow of the vital feel-good, unifying chemicals that run both our biology and our behaviour."[4]

When our founding moments are happy, our biology gets set up to assist us in having more happy moments. Unhappy founding moments create body chemistry that supports more unhappiness.

Major moments of trauma, because of their strong emotional energy, are especially influential in how we expect life to unfold and in what we attract to us. These moments of trauma may take us away from our natural alignment with our soul and therefore away from our most grace-filled possible life path.

In the first chapter, I mentioned two founding moments of emotional trauma that are common limitations to realizing and doing your full purpose. To recap, they were moments when, first, someone convinced you that their sensing and judgment were superior to your own inner sensing and, second, when you looked outside yourself to determine what to value and therefore what to do to receive the magic five (fame, fortune, power, love or approval).

These are just two examples of possible founding moments. Notice that the trauma is primarily on the emotional level. Trauma can happen on any level. Notice also that founding moments are so powerful that we actually believe the conclusions we reached at that time. And we keep believing them. And—this is the kicker—we attract more experiences that match our beliefs, and further convince us that our conclusions were accurate.

Let me give you an example to illustrate. Let's say you're William, the guy in chapter 2, who couldn't think of any moments of joy at work. He had lots of moments of joy in front of the computer. When you read his story you may have been asking yourself why he wasn't using his creative and technical computer skills to earn an income. Have you met anyone else that is great at something, yet they're not being that person in their paid profession? Here's why.

When William was six he was playing in the basement one day with his older sister and found his father's ham radio neatly tucked away on a shelf. He was naturally curious because he had always felt drawn to electronic devices. He pulled the radio off the shelf and placed it carefully on the floor. His curiosity overcame him and he strolled over to his father's workbench to grab a screwdriver and open up the radio to see what was inside.

Before he knew it—*sprong*!!!—all sorts of small parts were rolling across the cement floor. His sister found him and screamed, "Daddy's gonna kill you!" Then she ran upstairs to get her father. Daddy didn't kill him but it was pretty close. William got a slap on his buttocks and was sent to his room. He heard his father yelling as his sister took him off to his room, "That William is such a pest. He's always getting into things he shouldn't be touching. I wish he'd just stick to what I tell him to do."

This founding moment for William has physical, emotional, mental, and spiritual trauma. Physically, he feels the smack on his buttocks and his sister roughly pulling his arm as she guides him to his room. Emotionally he feels shame, fear, separation from his father, and anger that he's not understood. Mentally he decides "people don't understand me" and "I better just do what my father wants me to do." And spiritually he feels alone and abandoned. This hologram of experience on four levels gets wired into William's cells and his brain.

Then, because our bodies and minds are primarily vibrational, William begins to attract more experiences that reinforce what he felt and decided in that first founding moment. His world literally changes as he magnetizes more of the same. Eventually, he's forgotten that original moment and sees no connection when, at age twenty, he dreams about going to technical school and then decides, "I better follow my father's guidance. He knows better than I. I'll go to business school." This is the adult equivalent of the decision he made as a child to "just do what my father wants me to do." Soon he believes it's true. Someone else, in this case his father, knows better than he what he's meant to do.

The decisions he made in his founding moment pushed him away from his natural path. The only clues to his true path that remained were small moments of joy when he was doing more of the things to which he was naturally attracted.

This is an example of a young person's will being overpowered by an adult. It is a common type of founding moment. Please keep in mind that it is not always our parents who imprint those limiting moments. We are also profoundly affected by the thoughts, feelings and actions of everyone around us—the mass consciousness. And, through our Higher Self, we choose our parents and the experiences we will likely encounter. Therefore, please don't judge your founding moments. Use them as clues to heal and move forward. The first step is in recognizing your founding moments. Then you can set out to heal them.

What are some of the other founding moments that take us away from or move us towards our Soul Purpose?

Universal Founding Moments

Any issue that takes you away from the truth of your soul can take you away from your unique Soul Purpose. There are many and they have been categorized many different ways: as wounds, psychological disorders, steps around the native traditional medicine wheel, major character structures, etc. The universal founding moments that I list here are arranged so that you'll easily see their relationships to you and what holds you back or inspires you towards your purpose. I have described in detail only the limiting, or negative aspect, of each type of founding moment. The positive aspect is identified in brackets. Be looking for yourself in the descriptions and examples and write down any founding moments that apply to you.

No Choice (Versus Choice)

You experience that you have no choice on one or more of the four levels. You decide that this is just how it is.

No choice on the physical level may be, for example, being told you can't do something because of your physical capabilities, gender, race, or social status. You feel trapped in a body that limits your choices. For example, you are a young girl and your teacher tells you that girls aren't good at science. You believe her and allow your dream of becoming a world-famous chemist to dissolve. You choose a profession more acceptable to others. You feel you have no choice because you are a girl.

No choice on the mental level may occur when your beliefs about reality are challenged. For example, you may believe in your heart that you are a talented artist. However, people around you tell you your art is not good enough. You feel you have no choice about changing your thoughts about yourself.

Having no choice emotionally may stem from being told how you should feel. For example, you love rock music. The louder and more discordant the music, the better you like it. You listen to it whenever you can. Your father tells you it's *crap* and that you must be crazy to listen to it. You believe, on some level, that he must be right. You lose touch with your real feelings about the music as you take on the feelings that will bring your father's approval. You feel you have no choice about being *you*.

The spiritual level of *no choice* issues may take the form of feeling that God is stopping you from following your life's path because you are not worthy of God's support. For example, at age two you steal a toy from your brother. Your brother tells you that "God will get you for stealing" and "You're bad and you'll never go to Heaven." You believe the little stinker and shake in your boots. You form an opinion of yourself that God favours others over you because you're *bad*. Whenever things don't go your way, you remind yourself "This must be happening because I'm bad." You convince yourself you'll never be able to do what makes you happy because God thinks you're bad.

Power Over (Versus Power With)

You experience someone or something having power over you. You feel like a victim of someone else's will, or it may be that you believe it is God's Will that overpowers you.

At some level you begin to see the whole world as experiencing inequalities of power. Everyone is either a dominator or a victim. You vacillate between victim and dominator in each of your relationships. It seems as if these are the only roles that exist.

You can't even imagine having power *with* someone else. This may make it difficult to share things with others. You may experience great challenge in sharing living space with others. It feels as if someone has to always win and someone always loses.

Scarcity (Versus Abundance)

You experience a limit in resources such as time, love, or money. You decide, on some level, that there isn't enough for everyone or there isn't enough for you. You attract more experiences to match your beliefs. The groove gets deeper. It's not just a thought anymore—it's reality. Can't everyone else see it?

Limits on time: for example, your father was always busy with his job and never home. You feel that your purpose is to have children, yet you fear being as busy as your own father and unable to give your children what you missed out on. You feel stuck in the conflict of "There's not enough time to have a good job and give your children what they require."

Limits on love: for example, you felt you were never loved as a child. You experienced a lack of support in doing the things that mattered to you. You are still upset, and blame your parents for not giving you the love you felt you needed to do your life's work.

Limits on money: for example, all you heard as a child was that "there isn't enough money" to buy all the things or do all the things that your parents wanted. You took in this belief as if it was reality and it became part of your cells. You attracted experiences that matched that belief. When it came time to go to university you decided there just wasn't enough money to send you, and you could never earn enough yourself. You are blocked from seeking your purpose because of your limiting beliefs.

Doubting Your Truth (Versus Trusting Your Truth)

You lose touch with your natural ability to discern the truth. You believe that someone else knows more than you, and you look outside of yourself for answers. The power of your internal navigation system is lost as you continually set aside your own sensing and look to *experts* for the truth. You lose the freedom to express your true nature.

Separation (Versus Union)

You lose your connection with yourself, others, the Earth, or God.

Separation from Self

Disconnection from self is a common reaction to physical or emotional stress and trauma. If the body, on any level, is experiencing pain you step out of the body and disassociate with what it's feeling physically, emotionally, mentally, or spiritually.

When separation from the body becomes a common coping mechanism, you separate so much that you are unaware of what's happening physically and emotionally. The body's natural ability to give you immediate feedback to use in making choices becomes disabled.

Separation from Others
Separation from others may show up as feelings of being outside of the lives of others. You may put up shields so that others can't feel you and you can't feel them. You lose the natural intimacy and vulnerability that allows passion and power to feed and nurture close relationships.

Separation from the Earth
Separation from the Earth shows up as feeling ungrounded or disoriented. You may spend so much time in your head that you are out of synch with the natural rhythms of nature and the practical grounding available from the Earth. It may be difficult for you to bring things into concrete form to do your life's work. In other words, you have great ideas and feel that something always gets in the way of bringing the ideas into form.

Separation from God
You believe that God is outside of you. When other people describe spiritual experiences, you cannot relate. This may show up as a lack of faith in your ability to manifest anything powerful in your life—because you believe God creates and you are a bystander.

I'm Not Enough (Versus I'm Worthy)
This may show up as a decision that you are *stupid*, *less than*, or *without talent*. It affects your capacity to do your Soul Purpose because you may believe you lack the knowledge or intellect to

be something. For example, you love to help others and want to become a counsellor. But you decide that you're not smart enough, so you sell yourself short and become an administrative assistant to a counsellor instead. Whenever your dream comes into your mind you immediately cancel it out and remind yourself "I can't do that—I'm too stupid."

These are some of the classic founding moments that we share on a mass level. Individually we pick up and store combinations of these founding moments in our cells. The combinations form unique patterns in each of us. Some founding moments are universal, some hereditary, and some individual. In other words, there are some we all carry that have been stored within us from the first big bang, some that are unique to our family line, and some that are uniquely ours from our own experience. No matter where the founding moment came from, it is possible to heal the issue and let go of whatever is holding you back, on any level, from your Soul Purpose.

Jack picked up all six types of founding moments in his early childhood.

His mother consistently challenged his every thought and desire. He had an inner knowing that his thoughts and feelings about himself were accurate and yet he heard otherwise from his mother. He would sit in the kitchen with her as she quizzed him on his spelling. "Jack, how do you spell *turtle*?" "T – U – R – T – L – E." "No, that's not it!" Whack on the side of his head. He knew, inside himself, that he was right. Yet he turns the word over, again and again in his head, searching for the right answer. He's sure he gave the right answer.

He's confused and despondent (he doubts his truth), yet tries again to get the *right* answer. Again, she yells at him. He feels he has no choice (no choice). Either he pleases her or she gets upset with him. He feels rushed. If he gets the *wrong* answer she'll be mad at him (scarcity—limits on time and love). He can't win because *right* for her is not *right* for him. He doesn't realize that he can't get it right because she doesn't know the right answer herself. He feels she has power over him and he has no options but to try to make her happy (power over).

He loses his confidence in his own inner sense of who he is. He lacks the confidence to try again (he's not enough) to follow his own inner voice. So he doesn't develop any talents in his areas of true strength. To avoid the pain, he eventually disconnects from his own inner feelings (separation from self). Without his inner compass he's lost. Then, as an adult, he begins to look around him and realize that others have more choices. He's really angry. He wants to have his freedom back. He wants to heal.

Healing

Now that we've explored the types of founding moments that typically limit us in doing our Soul Purpose, let's explore what to do to heal the issues. Let me clarify what I mean by healing and say a little about the nature of healing in the world today. Healing is a big word. Healing is not therapy; it is transformation to a higher level. It is not awareness of your issues, traumas, or limitations; it is full release of these. Consider that all of your founding moments form pockets of energy that are wired into your cells. Each of these pockets contains thoughts, feelings, sensations, and beliefs that vibrate at a certain frequency, (like the frequencies of musical notes). The higher (more loving) the thought, feeling or belief, the higher the vibration. Healing, as I am referring to it here, means the total release, clearing, and transformation of a *founding moment*, on all levels. As you raise your overall vibration, you attract new experiences that match that new energy.

Let's get specific. Look for yourself in the following examples of healing so you can build your faith in your own capacity to change.

Here's an example of one man's founding moments and the healing that transformed them.

Duncan was the youngest of four children. Understandably, his mother was tired most of the time when she was breast-feeding him. He sensed that the other siblings were demanding and that each demand drained more life from his mother. He felt sorry for her and decided that he better keep quiet, take care of himself, and make as few demands as possible. After some time he became good at hiding his needs and feelings and putting others first. His founding moments included the issues of feeling limits on the time he could spend with his mother (scarcity, limits on time), as well as limits on the amount of love that was available to him (scarcity, limits on love). He disconnected from his own immediate feelings (separation from self) and put others first.

As an adult, Duncan could see that he missed out on opportunities to do his life purpose because he had difficulty asking for what he wanted. Throughout his life the issues created by the founding moments attracted similar experiences where Duncan seemed to put out a lot of love and to get less love back. He believed that other people just didn't have the same capacity to love as he did. In his work as a teacher he felt he put a lot of energy out and got few rewards.

The Healing Path

The healing for Duncan included some present-day coaching as well as revisiting childhood through regression. The intent of the regression for him was that he re-experience his past, identify the energy, on each level, that got wired in his cells, and then imprint a new, vibrationally higher experience. As Duncan's coach I helped him regress to a moment at six months old when he was breast-feeding in his mother's arms. He felt physically closed down and emotionally distressed because he could feel his mother's enormous physical stress from feeding and dressing all the other siblings for school after a late night working on other household chores. Mentally, he decided "It's better to close down and take nothing rather than stress her more and risk her getting sick." Spiritually, Duncan felt God was the only one present and available.

We called upon Duncan's Higher Self to assist him in accessing a higher vibrational experience to replace the feelings, decisions and energy of this early moment. I guided him to visualize and feel himself there in the new moment. He recreated by seeing his mother call upon her Higher Self for assistance with the other siblings. Several friends arrived to get the other kids off to school while his mother totally relaxed with him, playing, singing, and feeding him leisurely. Duncan felt his mother's body, mind, and heart relax and open as she felt nurtured by her connection to him. Duncan felt her love and strength and opened to receive it. His new decision was that it is great to open and receive from others and that there is an abundance of energy and love available to him from many people.

After several similar healing experiences, I followed up with some coaching about ways to bring the new beliefs and energies into the present. Duncan was asked to identify three people at work and three people in his social sphere who could assist him in doing more of the work he loved. He took some risks and expressed his needs, asking for assistance in ways he never would have in the past. He changed his response to the past and therefore changed his overall vibration. New opportunities presented themselves where he received a lot more support and assistance from his co-workers, boss, and friends than ever before. He got closer to doing the work he loves and more lined up with his Soul Purpose.

Here's another example of founding moments and the healing that transformed them. Roxanne's founding moments included issues of *power over, separation from self*, and *I'm not enough*. As a child she was repeatedly sexually abused by her father, and wired the experience on four levels:

- physically—pain in her stomach, pelvis and legs;
- emotionally—hurt, anger, sadness, shame, and revulsion towards sex;
- mentally—thoughts of *males hold power over females; I'm not worthy of love and caring; it's better to be out of my body than to feel sexually;* and *it's not OK to say what I really want, better to shut up, take the abuse, and stay mad so I don't attract more of it;*
- spiritually—feeling and thinking *God doesn't love me or he wouldn't allow this to happen.*

Roxanne knew that the abuse had affected her capacity to believe in herself and to attract jobs where she could express her natural talents in counselling, coaching, and valuing people. Her early childhood trauma had taken her away from her path of joy and fulfilment. She knew, on a deeper level, that there was some greater purpose in her life than what she was doing as an administrator for a clothing company.

As an adult, the founding moments stored in her cells caused her to attract experiences similar to those of her childhood. Her boss was controlling and used his power to bully people into overworking. She felt powerless to change her circumstances, and stayed too long in jobs and relationships where she felt undervalued, underutilized, stupid and ashamed.

Roxanne's most common emotional state was anger that stemmed from her fear of expressing her truth and being hurt. Most of her relationships ended in angry fights with unresolved pain. She believed that other people had all the power and that her best response, at work and socially, was to shut down, push people away with anger, and suffer through her situation, or leave.

Roxanne came for healing. We talked about her goals, wishes and dreams and the highest picture she could imagine for her life.

For Roxanne, healing involved revisiting those early childhood moments to change the energy she had stored on all levels. Her healing was managed in a similar way to Duncan's; however, it took longer. Where there are deeper emotional issues from harsher abuse, the healing cycle is often longer. The key with this type of healing is a firm, conscious belief that you are master of yourself on all levels and therefore capable of recreating yourself. Often, in healing situations where you are paying someone to help you change, that firm, conscious belief in your capacity to change comes originally from the healer and then gets transferred to the client.

I helped Roxanne to regress, with the intent that she re-experience her past, identify the energy, on each level, that got wired in her cells, and then imprint a new, vibrationally-higher experience. For example, we revisited a moment when her mother was out, and her father took her into her bedroom and fondled her. In that experience Roxanne felt physically nauseous, emotionally hurt by her mother for abandoning her, and spiritually separate from a God who would allow this to happen. Mentally, she decided that she had no power.

Using Roxanne's connection to her Higher Self we visualized a new, higher experience that Roxanne was guided to see and feel on all levels. The new experience featured her mother coming home during the abuse and being available to help Roxanne. Roxanne's Higher Self guided her in the bedroom to tell her father to stop touching her and to read her a book instead. In the new experience Roxanne felt safe physically and emotionally, and in control of her own power.

She recreated her father to be a caring, loving man who would honour her and read her a good book. Spiritually, in the recreation she felt God's loving presence urging her to take her power back. The interesting point about the recreation was that her mother didn't save her. She was just at home and available and totally ready to protect Roxanne if she needed help. Roxanne herself stopped her father from abusing her. This recreation restored Roxanne's full power because she believed that she was able to take charge of her own experience.

Soon Roxanne was taking back her power in her life's work. She felt more worthy and took risks to ask for jobs that were more responsible and fulfilling. She healed some of her past and got closer to the life path that felt more in alignment with her soul.

This description of healing may sound simplistic. When I describe the possibilities for healing in this way, some people respond with "How could it be so easy to change the past?" It is, and it isn't. It's easy in the sense that you absolutely can change the energy resulting from a past experience by revisiting and recreating it on all levels. It isn't easy in the sense that it requires a certain level of consciousness, willingness, and pure intent on the part of the healer and client for the full transformation to occur.

In working with Roxanne to help her get back on track with her Soul Purpose there was a clear and obvious link between her response to her childhood abuse and her current life circumstances. Often the link between childhood trauma and adult behaviour is not as obvious because the trauma seems too minor to affect beliefs and behaviour.

I've seen tremendous energy stored in founding moments that would seem to be unimportant at first glance. One woman lost her capacity to express herself at age two when she ran over to her father to tell him something just as he turned to answer the phone. She experienced that moment as rejection and decided that expression was unsafe. Who would believe that so much of our experience and how we perceive our lives is dependent on the thoughts, feelings, and stored energy of such a simple moment from early in life? As you are reflecting on your own life and founding moments, keep in mind that even *minor* events become founding moments when the emotional stakes are high.

In the next example we'll reconnect with William. He's the guy who shared his *Energetic-of-Soul Purpose* in chapter 2, and later the story of one of his founding moments. To recap, William's founding moment happened when he took apart his father's ham radio. His sister told on him and his father spanked him, yelled at him, and sent him to his room. William wired these energies in his cells: physically, sore buttocks and a sore arm where his sister dragged him upstairs; emotionally, he felt shame, fear, separation from his father, and anger about being misunderstood; mentally, he decided, "People don't understand me" and "I better just do what my father wants me to do"; and spiritually, he felt alone and abandoned.

In helping William to get back on the Soul Purpose track we did some regression work to clear that early childhood moment and change the vibration of his response. In recreating the experience, William linked up to his Higher Self and imagined his sister and father treating him differently. He still followed his natural curiosity and opened up the radio to explore inside. Instead of reacting by telling on William he saw his sister support him and say, "Don't worry William, I'll get Daddy and we'll put it back together."

Then his father arrived, smiled at William to acknowledge his curiosity, and knelt down to point out some of the things inside the radio. The recreation ended with William, his sister and father all bending over the radio to explore its components and put it back together as a team. William felt encouraged to be curious and excited about learning about electronics and how things work. On a spiritual level he now felt safe and more connected to his true self.

Following this and other healing experiences, William began to feel more confident about his dreams of using his natural curiosity and technical savvy to design and create computer games. He took a risk and applied for a job that would utilize his creative graphics skills and experience designing computer games. His life is now going down a new path because he transformed his energy, on all levels, and realigned his actions with his heartfelt intent.

You may be wondering what happens to the memories of the founding moments that get healed. One client described it this way: "The recreated moment now feels more real. I still remember the event as it originally happened, yet the memory becomes more clinical, more detached." Most people experience a change in their physiological response to the memory of the original event. Before the recreation, the memory brings up strong responses physically, emotionally, mentally, and spiritually. After the event has been healed and recreated they respond more strongly to the recreated moment, and the feelings and thoughts are much more pleasant and attractive.

The stories of Roxanne, Duncan, and William are just three examples of the ways in which our founding moments affect the reality we attract and create, and the healing that can transform it. I have given just a brief account of their issues and one example in each of their lives of a moment that was healed. Sometimes healing one issue related to life purpose will provide the opening for many areas of your life to change. Sometimes it takes healing of many moments, related to several founding moments, before your outer reality shifts. It all depends upon your personal timing, willingness, trust and faith, and the amount of energy still stored in those founding moments.

What I hope you will take away from these examples is the belief that you can fundamentally change, on all levels, and that the transformation can shift you closer to having a life you love.

The Speed Of Healing

Many people are realizing that the old paradigms about personal change no longer apply. What used to take years of weekly therapy can now happen in one session. This is not just because the *technology* of personal change has evolved; it is because we have all speeded up. We are vibrational, our issues are vibrational, and all energies on the planet, which also have a unique vibration, have been speeded up to encourage our evolution. Just look around at the information that is available to the average North American child. It has exploded exponentially over the last 20 years. What used to take hours of research can now happen in minutes over the Internet. The same explosion has happened in our cells.

Like most things that are sought after, we typically analyze them to death so we can duplicate them and sell them for a profit. In some ways true healing defies analysis and duplication because it spans all levels of being, even beyond what we are able to measure scientifically. How can you measure the amount of energy and life released through forgiveness? Is it possible to duplicate the amount of love a particular healer emits that allows forgiveness to be realized? How do you train someone in the humility it requires to truly let go?

Although I experience miracle after miracle of healing moments, where whole worlds shift, lives transform, and souls are reconnected to bodies, I can't promise you that there is a *technique* that heals. What I can offer is my experience, as well as my absolute faith, that healing will happen under certain conditions of the body, mind, heart, and soul.

Let me say upfront that I fully believe that the *new physics* is at work with all healing. The *new physics* shows us that our consciousness affects all levels of reality. Therefore, your consciousness about yourself, life, others, God, and healing also affects your capacity and speed of healing and transformation.

We heal with our hearts, minds, bodies, and souls. The true healers are not those who break you down into your individual parts; they work with all of you, on every level. Make healing a conscious part of your path towards your Soul Purpose.

FIVE

The Skills

OUR bodies are designed specifically, and magically, to allow us the greatest opportunity to manifest our Soul Purpose. As I said in chapter 1, creating your Soul Purpose requires skill in identifying what your body is feeling physically and emotionally, awareness of your thoughts, and conscious discernment about whether or not you are connected to your soul or Higher Self. Then, to attract opportunities to experience yourself doing your purpose requires the skill of magnetizing those situations, people, places, and things that perfectly match your *Energetic-of-Soul Purpose*.

In simple terms, this means we require the skills of sensing ourselves and our own highest truth (sensing energy) as well as the skill of sending out a frequency that the Universe can read to match us up with our purpose (sending energy). We are designed as vibrational beings with sending and receiving centres to do exactly these things. Our physical body is designed to easily link up with our emotional, mental, and spiritual bodies through the *energy body*, commonly called the *aura*. And within the *aura* are energy centres, called *chakras*, which function as our sending and receiving centres.

Our bodies give us instant feedback on our internal and external environment. We can sense our own feelings physically and emotionally, track our thoughts, and tune in to the spiritual realm with ease. We also send out vibrations, on all levels, that consciously or unconsciously attract a perfect match to what is going on inside. So the skills I'm going to outline here are really natural abilities; however, they are underdeveloped in most of us.

The skills are typically underdeveloped because many people are disconnected from their true feelings physically and emotionally and may be unconscious of their thoughts and how they are manifesting their reality. And, to a large extent, people ignore the highest truth from their soul. The reasons why many people are not in their bodies goes back to what we learned about change and trauma in chapter 4. Being out of your body is another way of saying you are ungrounded, disconnected, or *spacey*. In moments of intense physical, emotional, mental or spiritual trauma many people pop out of the body specifically so they will not feel the pain of what's going on.

They deny the messages of their soul for many more reasons, a few of which are listed here: the soul doesn't communicate through logic and most of us look for logic in decision-making; they disconnected from their soul early in life, believing that their spirit abandoned them in moments of pain; they were told by an authority figure that their true feelings and thoughts were *wrong* so they learned to discount their soul-felt emotions and ideas.

To recap, creating your Soul Purpose requires five skills:

1. Identifying what your body is feeling physically;
2. Awareness of what you are feeling emotionally;
3. Consciousness about what you are thinking mentally;
4. Conscious connection to your soul or Higher Self;

5. Consciously sending out a vibration to magnetize experiences of your *Energetic-of-Soul Purpose*.

Skill number five, *magnetizing*, has the next chapter all to itself.

Usually, when I list the skills of Soul Purpose, most people think they are doing them well already. Most people, for example, believe they are aware of their own thoughts.

In fact, most people are grossly unaware of what they are thinking or feeling on any level because they are not grounded and in their bodies. If you recorded their thoughts and played them back they would be astounded at the number of thoughts repeated in a day or week and the level of limitation in those thoughts. If you ask them what they are feeling they might respond by saying *fine* when, in fact, their bodies may be physically distressed or they may be holding emotions which have been unexpressed. Then, when I consciously guide them back into their bodies, they suddenly become aware of their true feelings. Often it is a surprise to them to feel what is really going on. A common reaction is "Wow, where did that come from? I had no idea I was feeling that way."

The first four skills of Soul Purpose have to do with reconnecting with yourself on all four levels of being. These skills of Soul Purpose, skills to reconnect with yourself, allow you to know your truth. You can only make decisions from the inside when you are able to discern what is true for you.

Some Guidelines For Reconnecting

Intent To Know The Truth
On a mental level, coming back into connection with your body, mind, and spirit requires conscious intent to know the truth. This may sound simple and easy. It is easy to say and intend, and not

so easy to implement. It requires willingness to know your truth and to act on what you know. The acting-on-it part is what is challenging. And the *knowing* and *acting* parts go hand in hand. In other words, once you know the truth you can no longer deny what you are thinking, feeling, and being; then it becomes more uncomfortable to not act.

Let me give you some examples where you can identify your own denial and disconnection from the truth. Let's say you dislike visiting with your family. You find your mother bossy and controlling, or your father is too dominant or a wimp. Your brother-in-law addresses you with controlled disdain and comments on your *simple tastes*, which you interpret as meaning that you are less sophisticated than he. Insert whatever dislikes and judgments you feel for the various members of your family or in some other area of your life.

In order to visit with them you have to dissociate from your true feelings. After awhile you master the ability to step outside your true feelings with your family (or co-workers or friends) and you find yourself *tolerating* the visits. You are so out of touch with your own body, heart, mind, and spirit when you're with them that you cannot feel yourself or them. It feels like *eating air* when you're with them—you can't remember what it tasted like or how you felt while eating it. You think you don't care anymore. You say to yourself, "I don't care whether or not I ever see them again."

You are in denial of your true feelings because you have chosen to step out of your body so you don't feel anything. Doing stage one of Soul Purpose skill development in this example means consciously choosing to know the truth of what you are experiencing when you're with your family and then climbing back in the body to experience your truth.

Here's another example of denial and disconnection. Let's say you're married with two children. Your husband never seems happy when he's at home. He certainly never seems happy to see you. He is often depressed, and yells at the kids. You are so sick of the arguments between him and the children. It feels like you're always putting out fires at home. You feel uncared-for, unloved, and alone. You tell yourself you're staying in the marriage for the kids and because your husband would be lost without you. You've never told anyone how unhappy you're feeling and how much you want out.

Overall, you feel empty. How can you get in touch with any passion for a job when your home life seems so unreal? You're sure this is not your life purpose. The emptiness is disconnection from true feelings. The only way to safely move forward is to get in touch with your true feelings and to act on them with love. This means love for yourself first, and love for others. Again, stage one of Soul Purpose skill development is choosing to feel your truth, and then reconnecting on all levels to discern the right actions.

How To Get Back In

Once you decide you want to be in touch with your truth you need to get back into your body to feel what's going on. At the level of intent, start by promising yourself that you will be willing to feel and know what is true for you. In the example above, of visiting family or friends, set an intention that will assist you in climbing back into your body. A powerful intention may be written down as follows: *to be consciously aware, on all levels, of the truth of my feelings and thoughts in order to be in my body, in the present moment, with the greatest capacity to discern my truth.* Often just setting the intention takes you a long way towards realizing your goal of reconnection.

In addition to intent there are many practical tools and techniques for re-entry. All of them require the discipline to practice sensing and feeling what's going on physically, mentally, emotionally, and spiritually. It often takes from six to twelve months to get good at checking in with yourself and scanning the inner landscape to know your truth. One method that I find helpful was taught to me by Gordon-Michael Scallion and Cynthia Keyes.[5] It is a simple, yet powerful meditation to reconnect to spirit, the Earth, and yourself. I have adapted it in Appendix 2 for grounding and reconnecting.

Reconnecting Physically

In general, the things that help you get back into your body are grounding experiences coupled with conscious tuning in to the physical level. Here's a list of things you can do more regularly to reconnect physically:

- Eat sufficient amounts of protein—protein is grounding, yet many people skip protein altogether or have it just once a day. Try it three times a day in balance with carbohydrate and fat intake.
- Exercise—walking is grounding and a good, basic form of body movement. Find some form of exercise to do and use it to reconnect.
- Move your sexual energy through lovemaking, tantra exercises[6] or Qi Gong.[7] Sexual energy is the same energy as healing energy. It is beneficial to learn to feel where the energy is in your body and to learn to spread it around to places where the energy is more stagnant.
- Get good rest and sleep.
- Balance the use of your body, mind, and spiritual connection.

As you practice any of these, focus your mind on enhanced awareness of your body sensations. Notice temperature changes and flow of energy through the body, feelings of heaviness or lightness, changes in tension and relaxation, and inflow and outflow of energy.

With practice you'll be able to discern the kinds of things that help you stay in touch with your body and cause you to disconnect. Keep in mind that the various levels—physical, emotional, mental, and spiritual—are not separate. The kinds of things that bump you out or help you stay in may be emotional, mental, or spiritual also. You'll begin to notice how the various levels affect each of the others.

Reconnecting Emotionally

Reconnecting emotionally is assisted by any of the things you do to reconnect physically. Your emotions are the feelings that arise in your body. They either feel *expanding* and we call them positive, or they feel *contracting* and we call them negative. Positive emotions are the ones we say we like. Negative emotions are the ones we say we don't want.

Another way of looking at the positive/negative emotion continuum is to label them higher vibrational or lower vibrational emotions. Lower vibrational emotions are ones like resentment, grief, or anger. Higher vibrational emotions are joy, forgiveness and love. By thinking of them as having a certain vibration, you introduce the concept of changing the vibration. Just knowing that you can transform your emotions often helps in reconnecting with them.

We often judge negative emotions and sometimes push them away. It is possible to have an emotion in your body and not feel it. This is called denial. It may be conscious or unconscious denial. If you were out of your body during an intense, emotional moment, it is likely that you did not feel the emotions in that moment.

It takes courage to reconnect with your emotions. It will be easier if you can tell yourself *not* to judge what you find. An emotion that is judged has a difficult time moving out of the body. Here's a list of things you can do to reconnect with your emotions:

- Reconnect physically—be willing to know what you are feeling emotionally by being in your body.
- Be in a place of non-judgment—emotions are just emotions. They are not good or bad; they are just what you are feeling.
- Remind yourself that YOU HAVE CHOICE ABOUT WHAT YOU FEEL—you can transform the emotion to something higher.
- Learn to distinguish one emotion from another. What is the difference between grief and sadness, joy and happiness? Each of them will feel a little different in the body. Build a bank of information about each emotion and how it feels physically for you. You may want to write down the emotions and their corresponding physical sensations.

Reconnecting Mentally

Reconnecting mentally means being aware of your thoughts. Pause right now. What were you just thinking? Often there is more than one conversation happening in your mind. You may be processing what you are reading at the same time as you are fantasizing about recreating a wonderful moment or struggling with a current problem.

Thoughts move in quickly and may take you away from your current, conscious place of focus. Thoughts are creative. Everything we bring into form started out as an idea. By being aware of your thoughts you can direct them towards the future you choose to create.

There is usually a direct relationship between the quality of your thoughts and the quality of your experiences. The moment something appears to *go wrong* in a particular area of your life, ask yourself, "What have I been thinking about in that area of my life?" For example, let's say you want a better job, with more responsibility. It doesn't happen. All you get are job offers with the same or less responsibility. Ask yourself, "What are my thoughts about *more responsibility*?" You may find that you think you are incapable of handling greater responsibility. Your thought has kept you from manifesting what you say you want.

Here's a list of tips to help you be conscious of your thoughts:

- Track your thoughts in areas where you are unhappy. Notice the thoughts that may be limiting you from having what you say you want. Write them down. Think of new, higher thoughts to replace them.
- Use positive affirmations. As you think of what you want to be saying to yourself, you will become aware of the thoughts that are in the way. Refer to *Creative Visualization*[8] for some ideas.
- Practice pausing and noticing your thoughts throughout the day. I use this when the phone rings or when an unexpected event occurs. I check in with myself and notice what I was thinking just before it happened. This trains you to be aware of the connections between your thoughts and what you attract.

Reconnecting Spiritually

Reconnecting spiritually requires practice, just as reconnection on all other levels. Any of the traditional spiritual practices will work as long as you have true intent to connect. You can use meditation, prayer, *seva* (work that is a service to spirit), chanting, song, dance, or running. Basically, choose whatever does it for you.

Don't be too fanatical about the *how*, just focus on the intent to connect. There is more than one way to meditate, and meditation is not the only way to connect spiritually. It may work better for you to keep a schedule for reconnecting so that your body knows "OK, at 7 a.m. we pray." Training your nervous system to connect spiritually at the same time each day will make reconnecting easier.

Piggyback your spiritual practice on the strong connections of others. Listen to audiotapes, read books, or listen to music that holds a high, spiritual connection for you. Do things with others that will assist you in connecting. The prayers and meditations in chapter 8 of *Soul Purpose* are offered as a place to start building your spiritual practice. There are also some good ideas in *It's a Meaningful Life*[9] by Bo Lozoff. Start here, then design your own.

Here are some guidelines to help you reconnect spiritually:

- Connect to your Higher Self daily. Ask for help. Chapter 8 will assist you in bringing your Higher Self down to Earth.
- Thank your Higher Self for what's working.
- Talk to spirit as if you believe it is listening. Whether it's your Higher Self, God, angels, devas, your spirit guides, or a deceased relative—know that they do exist and are aware of your words.
- Don't wait until you *need* spirit to connect. Make it a daily practice and do it!
- Find a way to have fun. For Heaven's sake, it doesn't have to be serious! You won't believe how humourous your spirit guides can be. If your Higher Self is like mine you'll be on the floor laughing.

Cautions About Re-entry

Don't be surprised if you feel different from your usual self once you're reconnected to your body. You may feel like you are heavier, more tired, and generally more sensitive to everything. You are not really heavier, you're just feeling the heaviness of everything you are carrying around that may have been unfelt up till now. You are not more tired; you're just feeling the physical, mental, or emotional fatigue that has been unfelt. And, of course, you'll be more sensitive because you're now back inside, feeling all the many shades of emotions, physical sensations, and spiritual inspirations that your body is designed to sense and feel.

I recognize that you may be feeling some *overwhelm* at this point. "You mean I have to do this to reconnect physically, and this and that to reconnect emotionally. Then I have to track my thoughts at the same time as I work on a spiritual practice!?" Yes, I do mean that it is going to take focus, intention and energy for you to get back in touch with yourself on all levels. If you are choosing your Soul Purpose then you are choosing to BE HERE and consciously experience life. Here's the carrot...

...*it works*.

Know yourself. Know what truly brings you happiness. Reconnect on all levels. Then create a life where you're being happy. The next chapter tells you how to do the creating.

SIX

Magnetizing

Your Soul Purpose

*The real test of all spiritual work is not whether you
have had a conscious experience of your soul,
but how your life is expressed in the everyday world
—with family, friends, and co-workers.*

LaUna Huffines
BRIDGE OF LIGHT[10]

You have now done the research to allow you to know, inside and out, your personal *energetic*. The next step is to put this information to work—to magnetize your Soul Purpose. You will be guided through the steps to take what you have learned about yourself in chapters 2 and 4 and turn it into a powerful magnet to attract the people, situations, healing and learning opportunities to prepare you, and support you in repeating the experience of your personal *energetic* over and over again.

You have already been reminded that your path may not be a straight line. You will attract the opportunities to evolve and raise your vibration through healing. In addition, you will learn skills and gain experiences to allow you to take in joy more deeply.

This chapter would not have been possible without experiences on my own path that helped me to see all of the levels that we access when we manifest. I am indebted to the pioneers that have researched and written about manifesting. My journey accelerated when I read *Think and Grow Rich*[11] by Napoleon Hill. His genius is in the fact that his process focuses on all four levels. Another teacher who gave us more pieces of the manifesting puzzle was Shakti Gawain in *Creative Visualization*.[8] Next, I found Jess Stearn's *The Power of Alpha-Thinking*[12] and Sanaya Roman and Duane Packer's *Creating Money*.[1] And, in the last few years, I learned from God in Neale Donald Walsch's *Conversations with God*[2] series.

I immediately put the ideas from the books into practice in my own manifesting rituals and in my coaching of clients. Again, I learned quickly that the first thing you often manifest is your healing. I also learned the profound lessons of the power of the unconscious mind to thwart our conscious attempts to manifest. It doesn't matter how often you affirm *I am an abundant child of the Universe*, or how frequently you visualize yourself receiving a cheque for twelve million dollars. If your unconscious mind holds a different belief and/or a different picture, you will not manifest what you say you want.

This is when I started to research hypnosis and other tools to access the unconscious. I was surprised to learn that hypnosis merely means that your brain is in an altered state of conscious awareness where the brain activity slows down to the *alpha* state. The power of hypnosis is with the person who enters the hypnotic state, not with the facilitator. Since we all access alpha on our way to and from sleep, this seems like a natural time to use self-hypnosis to guide the unconscious and conscious minds to align with the new *energetic*. Now I had all the pieces of the manifesting process to put you on the fast track to living your *energetic* every day.

Keys To Manifesting

Keep in mind that all of life, as we know it consciously, exists on four basic levels: physical, emotional, mental and spiritual. Therefore, to manifest consciously you must be aware of and be consciously focused on all four levels. Then, as we learned above, you must be in control of the conscious and unconscious minds and align them on the four levels. Sounds like a lot of juggling! Don't despair. I will guide you through the steps that have proven to work for myself, the clients who have followed them, and others who have learned from the pioneers.

In this chapter, I will guide you in consciously choosing what you want to be experiencing on each of the four levels. Then you will tie this together with your description of your *Energetic-of-Soul Purpose* as far as you can see it and feel it right now. You will learn a meditation for powerful manifesting, using your personal *energetic* that you have developed through this book. In chapter 8 and the appendices, you'll receive some prayers, affirmations, and a self-hypnosis transcript that will assist you in further manifesting by aligning your unconscious mind with your conscious choices.

Let's begin manifesting right away by focusing on who you choose to be and consciously recreating you on four levels.

Choosing How To Be
In *Friendship with God*[3] Neale Donald Walsch asks God,
    "Can't I simply choose to be happy?"
    And God responds, *Yes*.

Then Neale asks, "How? How do I do that?"

And God responds,

*Don't do it. Simply be it. Do not try to **do** happy. Simply choose to **be** happy, and everything you do will spring from that. It will be given birth by that. What you are being gives birth to what you are doing. Always remember that.*

This is the first task—choosing how to be. It is the simplest, and the most challenging to teach. It requires letting go of the mass-consciousness belief that there is a doing thing that will make us happy and that we won't be happy until and unless we are doing that thing. You have choice about what you are going to *be*. You may choose to be *happy*. You may choose to be *loving*. You may choose to be *fulfilled*. You may choose all of these things and more.

Choosing how to be also requires that you take full responsibility for yourself and what you are experiencing. This is big. No, this is HUGE! It means that you master the capacity to create how you are being and to keep choosing that state of being no matter what happens. So, for example, you choose to take on the state of being which we call *happy*. You choose, on all levels, to *be happy*. Then, you go out into the world and take that state of being with you and stay in that state regardless of the way that the world interacts with you.

This means that you do not judge what you attract; you merely observe it as a reflection of some aspect inside of you that surfaces as you are *being happy*. It may be your healing of a doubt or fear from the past. It may be a possible future you projected from your unconscious mind. Whatever it is, you accept it and still choose to *be happy*. And if happy is not how you choose to be, then you change to the next state of being that is consciously chosen.

So far this sounds like a lot of philosophy. Let's translate this into the world most of us experience.

You decide that you are going to *be happy*. You head out to be happy so you can get this manifesting skill under your belt and get on with your Soul Purpose. You go to work and your boss tells you it will be necessary to work late. You find yourself losing that state of *happy* as it transforms into *resentful*, *angry*, and *powerless*. You catch yourself in the transformation and make a conscious choice: "No, I'm choosing to be happy," and you take the actions that align with that choice.

You take full responsibility. "I chose this job. I've stayed even though I know there is a lot of overtime work. I know my boss rewards people for wearing themselves out." You do not judge. "That is a choice my boss has made. I don't agree, yet I accept that's her choice. I know that this company seeks profits first and gives lip service to employee satisfaction." You choose to *be happy*. "I choose to be happy. I'll stay tonight and then I'll begin tomorrow to manifest a job more closely aligned with my values."

In relationship to magnetizing your Soul Purpose, task one is choosing how you want to be. The natural *doing* will fall out of that. Let's say you're Samantha from chapter 2. She is an assistant to the sales manager at a car dealership. She might choose to be *loving* as a first step in magnetizing her purpose.

Choosing Your Physical Experience

The second task is consciously describing the physical experience you choose to create. You can describe this to yourself at the essence level, meaning that you outline the essence of the experience and leave the specifics up to spirit. Or, you can be specific and describe the colours, fabrics, smells, tastes, and numbers of chairs in your visualization. Either way works well, as long as you focus on how you'll be feeling and being in the physical environment. This is what the Universe focuses on in magnetizing—your felt response to the environment.

For Samantha from chapter 2, the physical experience she enjoyed was to feel physically relaxed and energized. She wanted to be in a physical environment that was comfortable, like her home.

Choosing What You'll Think

This is the third task. You use the information from the personal research of your *energetic* to pick the thoughts about yourself, others, the world, and your life that support magnetizing the moments of joy. Samantha might choose to think, "I am a loving person. People appreciate my thoughtfulness. I easily attract situations where my people-skills are valued."

One way to tune in to the thoughts that would be most helpful is to ask yourself what thoughts you hold that are limiting, then consciously choose thoughts that hold the opposite vibration. For example, let's say you often think like William in chapter 2. He held the thought that his father knew better than he what he was good at and should focus on. In consciously choosing new thoughts to manifest his purpose, William could say to himself, "I have a powerful sense of what is right for me. My choices serve me on all levels. I value my own discernment while opening to the wisdom around me." These new thoughts would hold a higher vibration for William and assist him in attracting experiences that matched those new thoughts.

Projecting How You'll Feel

The fourth task is adding the emotions you choose to feel as you are living your Soul Purpose. As you imagine yourself being happy and fulfilled, feel the emotions in your body that match what you want to create. For Samantha, who has chosen to be loving and to think of herself as attracting situations where her skills are valued, she may choose to feel valued, appreciated, and loving about herself and others. In projecting how you will feel as a part of magnetizing your purpose, it is important to imagine yourself in your body feeling the things you are projecting.

Imagining Your Spiritual Connection

Connecting on the spiritual level may seem more challenging for some of you. One of the easiest ways to imagine your spiritual connection is by tuning in to a person, place, or thing that moves you on that level and using that as your grounding to spirit. For example, if you have a spiritual teacher or have faith in a particular saint, angel, or divine being, tune in to them and imagine them beside you. If you associate prayer or connection to a place, such as a temple, church, or personal alter, imagine yourself there and feel how it would feel in your body.

For some people, just asking for a picture or symbol of their Higher Self immediately connects them to spirit. For others, a visualization using light often helps. Here's an example: Sit quietly in a comfortable position. Imagine a net of light attached to the back of your head that reaches all the way up to the spiritual level. Imagine climbing the net to find and be with your Higher Self and personal guides. As you reach the top of the net, imagine climbing off and stepping onto solid ground on the spiritual level. See a large round table in front of you. As you sit down at the table, imagine your Higher Self sitting right across from you gently gazing at you as you make eye contact. On either side of your Higher Self see a personal guide or guardian angel. Tune in to the energies of each of them and feel how that feels in your body. Scan your body and take note of areas that feel open, closed, hot, or cold. Write down what you see and feel. Use the visualization when you need to reconnect for manifesting.

Freeing Up Space

The final component of magnetizing is ensuring that there is space in your life for new things to come in and *land*. You must create space, on all levels, for new things by letting go of what's not working and no longer serves your higher purpose. This means letting go of old ideas about yourself, limiting beliefs about the world and actions that are inconsistent with being the person you choose to be. Healing will do some of this and you must also back up the healing by creating time in your life for new experiences.

Tom and Alia wanted to have a child. They were both busy salespeople with tight schedules and little free time. Their days off were packed with errands, visiting, and generally more *busyness*. Where was there any room for the many, many demands of a newborn child? Through healing they realized that they had allowed themselves to be driven by their need to feel successful in the eyes of others. They chose to consciously create more space for a baby, and changed their lives to strike a more nurturing balance of work, play, leisure, and spiritual reconnection.

Preparing To Manifest Your Soul Purpose

Let's put the manifesting steps together now so you can practice using your *energetic* to attract opportunities to be aligned with your Soul Purpose. Go back over your answers to the first nine questions about your *energetic* and your summary description from chapter 2.

Choosing How To Be

Reflect on the information you have now for your *Energetic-of-Soul Purpose*. How do you choose to be? Which Universal Energies do you choose to express? It can be as simple as *being happy* or *loving* or *joyous*. Keep in mind that Soul Purpose is an ever-evolving process. What you choose to focus on being today will transform over time. Write down the word that best captures how you choose to be right now.

Choosing Your Physical Experience

As you reflect on your summary description of your *Energetic-of-Soul Purpose* you will notice a lot of data about the physical environment, the people, sights, sounds, words, and things you love to be around. Reflect on this now and write out a description of the physical experience you choose to create. Enhance it and embellish with your greatest dreams for your Soul Purpose. Imagine how you'll feel physically being in your ideal environment.

Choosing What You'll Think

Pause and ask yourself what thoughts you choose to hold about yourself that will assist you in manifesting your purpose. Go back over your answers to the first nine questions about your *energetic*. What thoughts about yourself, life, others, and your soul would support being in this perfect *energetic*? Tune in to the thoughts that would be most helpful by asking yourself what thoughts you hold that are limiting, then consciously choose thoughts that hold the opposite vibration. As you think about doing your life's purpose, what limiting thoughts arise? Write them down. Now, turn the thoughts around and raise their vibration by creating new thoughts that would balance these limiting ones. Write these new thoughts down.

Projecting How You'll Feel

Imagine yourself fully connected to your Soul Purpose. Again, tune in to what you are choosing to be. Say to yourself, "I am choosing to be _____ " (insert your words). You may choose to be happy, loving, fulfilled, self-actualized, abundant. It's up to you how you choose to be.

Think of the feelings you choose to have when you are what you've chosen to be. How do you choose to feel about yourself, others, the world, and spirit? Write down those feelings that most closely align with the thoughts you choose to hold about yourself. Take them to their highest vibration. For example, if you choose to feel cared-for, take that one notch higher and choose to feel valuable, cherished, nurtured and loved. Project the highest feelings you can access. Write down a list now that captures the feelings you choose to manifest.

Imagining Your Spiritual Connection

Use one of the techniques above to connect to your soul. Pause and tune in to your body, mind, and emotions. What are you feeling and thinking? How does it feel in your body? As closely as possible, capture this in words and write it down for future reference. The more often you tune in and sense what's going on internally the better you'll be able to describe the experience and use it to manifest powerfully.

Now we'll put all the steps together using a vibrational meditation that will help you to focus on all levels of being in manifesting opportunities to do your *energetic*. This meditation was inspired by the book *Creating Money*,[1] by Sanaya Roman and Duane Packer. It teaches how to create, using energy and magnetism. I have used this meditation numerous times with clients and workshop groups. Of all the manifesting tools I've come across, this one packs the biggest spiritual punch. We learn how to attract the highest experiences quickly and gracefully as we manifest our Soul Purpose.

The most important aspect of the exercise is your feeling of personal power. I recommend using your connection to your Higher Self because it has proved effective in giving people the experience of power. Feel free to adapt the visualization to what works best for you in feeling magnetic. Remember, your body is designed to create. This exercise guides you in using your natural manifesting abilities to reconnect on all levels and create the life you choose. You may want to record the exercise on tape and play it back while you're in a relaxed state. Be creative and inventive—it's your life!

Soul Purpose Magnetizing Exercise

1. Sit comfortably in a quiet spot that feels safe and encourages you to open. Close your eyes, relax, and tune in to your body by focusing on your heart centre. Using all of the information that you have accessed so far about your *Energetic-of-Soul Purpose*, and how you choose to be on all four levels, imagine yourself aligning with your purpose. Think positively about being able to do your Soul Purpose. Know that it is possible and that you have the power to attract what you require. See and feel yourself attracting the Universal Energies you are choosing to express.

2. Visualize the experience you choose to have and make it as real as possible. Be with your body and imagine how you will feel physically. Describe it to yourself as you actually feel it in your body and experience your response. Focus on your overall intent. What are you consciously creating for yourself and others?

3. Think of the thoughts you will hold about yourself. Say them in your mind now. Choose for these thoughts to become your truth about yourself.

4. Imagine how you will feel emotionally. Scan through your list of emotions in your mind and feel each of them in your body right now. Feel yourself open as your feelings increase in vibration and move you towards your highest potential.

5. Imagine your spiritual connection as you are doing your purpose. Experience it in your body as you imagine yourself on the spiritual level. Consciously connect to your Higher Self and ask for assistance in magnetizing.

6. Now consciously imagine the exchange you choose to have with others, your environment and soul. Feel how good it feels to give and receive. Imagine the exchange on four levels. Experience how your body feels as the exchange is occurring.

7. As you imagine and experience yourself in your *Energetic-of-Soul Purpose*, feel yourself becoming magnetic to the people, places, things, and experiences that will easily allow you to manifest your purpose. To do this, draw a beautiful white light into the top of your head and down through your heart and into your solar plexus. Imagine your powerful Higher Self standing behind you, sending this stream of light out into the world. See the light glowing brightly as it moves away from your solar plexus and travels out into the world. Continue to channel the white light through the top of your head and out of the solar plexus as you see the light spread across your geographical area. Send it out as far as you wish to go in attracting the people, places, and circumstances for you to manifest your Soul Purpose.

8. Use your imagination and adapt the colour and intensity of light so that it feels powerful in attracting your Soul Purpose. You are now generating a magnetic force field that will attract what you are choosing.

9. As the light spreads out, imagine it's like a large net spreading out and drawing to you what you require. As you attract what you want, discern where to bring it into your energy. Does it feel appropriate to bring it into a certain area of your body? Does it feel better to see it surrounding all of you? Do you see it entering your hands so you can work with it to further manifest? Whatever feels right for you will work best in your manifesting process.

10. As the stream of light builds energy, tune in to the healing and learning that will be required before you are doing your Soul Purpose. There may be a number of steps along the way to guide you towards your purpose. You can control the speed at which you do the healing and learning by speeding up or slowing down the sequence of events. Get in touch with the overall plan. Feel how it feels to you right now. Is it moving too quickly or too slowly? Play with the rate of events until it feels comfortable for you.

11. Continue to channel energy into your stream of light as long as it feels right for you. You will get a sense when you have done enough magnetizing. Learn to play with the energy until you are using just enough to magnetize what you desire without overextending yourself or sending out too little energy to draw what you require. Each time that you magnetize may feel a little different, with some experiences feeling powerful and others feeling less so.

Tune in to the best moments to magnetize when you feel drawn to create.

12. Check in on how often to magnetize. It may be once a day, or three times per week, for example. You'll get a sense of what feels right.

13. Continue to magnetize and write down any insights that come to you. Act on the inspiration you receive. The more you act on the messages you receive the more inspiration you'll attract.

Freeing Up Space

End with this step by scanning your life and asking yourself whether you have room to experience your *Energetic-of-Soul Purpose*. Start with where you are, and look for opportunities to maximize your potential to be in the *energetic* as soon as possible. One quick way to free up space is to ask yourself what you do not enjoy doing and plan to stop those activities right away. Stop yourself if your mind intervenes to tell you why you have to keep doing the things you don't enjoy. Call your life into question. If it doesn't feel good and you're not being the person you choose to be, why do it? It may take some time to reorganize your life with more space for your Soul Purpose. Start right away by creating some free time for fun, fulfilment, and joy, and trust that the Universe will bring that to you with ease.

Stories of Soul Purpose

Having the formula, tools, and techniques for creating your Soul Purpose means nothing if they don't work. Let me tell you some real-life stories to increase your confidence. Keep in mind that this is an ever-evolving process. You never arrive; you continually create. Each of the people in these stories is much further along their Soul Purpose path, yet they may go still further.

Deb was out of work. She knew she didn't want to be experiencing the undervaluing she had felt in all of her previous jobs. In every situation she seemed to attract bosses who abused their power. She had held positions in retail sales, office administration, and bookkeeping. She knew inside that her purpose had more to do with helping people grow—something she had learned from the inside through her own personal growth.

Deb spent some time doing the inner healing work and decided to clear some issues where she gave other people her power. She interviewed friends to understand her gifts and get clearer about her ideal *energetic*. It took time, and a huge investment of trust in the process of healing. She magnetized a great new job in an enlightened company and experienced feeling valued and being *seen* in ways she never before imagined. Her job evolved over time and she found herself helping others grow. She knew she was closer to her purpose.

Lee is a successful businesswoman. She has held executive positions as vice-president or president of major corporations. She has all the trappings of outer success and she is a happy person. Following her departure from her last corporate role she decided that she wanted to *check in* with herself and more consciously create her next role to be closer to her Soul Purpose. She used the steps to identify her *Energetic-of-Soul Purpose* and realized that she had created situations where she was living the *energetic* in part. However, she could see that there was some healing in the way of her living it completely.

Her *energetic* included helping others to recover and use their personal power at work, and using her compassion, energy, inspiration, and humour to facilitate and educate others to transform their workplaces and make them more *human*, real, and effective. She had created situations where she was living this part of her *energetic*.

What was missing was being in environments where the leaders were comfortable with the amount of power Lee shared with her employees. To live in her ideal *energetic* she wanted to spend more of her time inspiring more people where her values were understood and wanted. Through healing and reflection on the ideal *energetic* to magnetize, she became clearer about what she wants to create. She now has the awareness and tools to attract situations that are closer to her *energetic*. Experiences are now coming to her that help her change her thoughts about what's possible so she can live her Soul Purpose.

Paul was working in organization development for a large company. He did training, facilitating and individual consulting. He felt blessed to be helping other people develop their leadership qualities and improve their job skills. Even though he felt successful and secure, he became unhappy.

Because of his learning about personal growth he recognized the unhappiness not as a *bad* thing, but as a signal to make changes. He did some personal healing and let go of limiting thoughts about what was possible. He recognized that his true desire was to have his own business. His father had lost money several times in bad investments. To be comfortable he'd have to clear his beliefs that successful business people often make mistakes and fail.

He did the healing and got clear on his *energetic*. He chose to start a spiritually-based company that helped people to position themselves for greater success. He took a risk and left the security of his job. Today he runs his own business successfully and feels he's doing his Soul Purpose.

7
SEVEN

Bringing

Your Higher Self To Earth

IN many ways the end result of getting to Soul Purpose is a closer connection to your soul or Higher Self. I like to think of it as raising your vibration so much that your soul just pops into your body and stays down here with you. In other words, the part of you that is connected to God, your Higher Self, is the aspect of you that has been encouraging you all along to follow your true purpose. Your Higher Self is totally loving, totally aware of all aspects of you, and able to draw to you everything that you require to heal, learn and grow towards your purpose. Therefore, anything that you can do to bring your Higher Self to Earth faster will speed up the process of achieving your Soul Purpose.

Your Higher Self comes to you all the time with a higher possibility for every moment. Its goal is to support you on your pathway to purpose by inspiring you to *take the high road*. This is the option in every circumstance that would be the highest, most loving choice. It is not necessarily the most logical choice.

Ellen used to work in research. She has an analytical mind and a thirst for knowledge. She became interested in natural healing and took a course in massage. Her teacher was arrogant and instructed the women in the class to remove their tops for their treatments with other students. Some of them were male. Ellen and the other women were enraged, but she was the only woman who spoke out against the inappropriateness of the request. Her anger soon turned to rage when she was told that she "had to obey" the request or forfeit her course fees and leave.

Her rage may have taken her off of her path and away from *the high road*. However, she checked in with her Higher Self through prayer and meditation. She was guided to ask the opinion of many other healers, friends, and professionals. Rather than acting on her unloving thoughts of revenge and conflict she sought counsel to find balance in her response.

Ellen decided to leave this massage training centre and study with a teacher who honoured and respected her higher path to learning without discomfort and unfairness towards women. Although she lost some money, she also learned to respect her initial instinct to be wary of the first instructor from the beginning. What she gained in self-respect and faith outweighed the financial losses. By connecting to and acting with her Higher Self she chose a higher path and got closer to her Soul Purpose. Remember, the path itself is your Soul Purpose, not just the end result.

Often, the choices on *the high road* of your Higher Self will not make sense. However, when you are tuned in to your Higher Self, the messages you receive will feel more loving, more open and expansive in your body. Take the time to tune in, be in your body, and check in on how your inner messages feel when you imagine following the guidance. Soon you'll develop an inner database of the feelings that tell you you're connected and on track in discerning the difference between your logic and your intuitive sense.

Raising Your Vibration

In order to create a *container* for your Soul to stick around and keep you on the high road, you may want to actively raise your vibration. What does this mean in practical terms? As I said earlier, all aspects of you have vibration. Your physical body holds energy and vibration. Each of your feelings has a particular frequency. Your thoughts are either high or low in vibration, and your spiritual connection may be nonexistent, low or high. Together, these four levels create your overall vibratory rate. The sum total of all those vibrations creates a frequency that makes you magnetic to more experiences of the same vibration.

Your Higher Self is always with you; however, you'll be better able to hear, feel, or sense the messages and promptings of your soul if your thoughts and feelings are already at a higher vibration. Let's get specific.

A thought such as *life sucks* is at a much lower vibration than a thought such as *life is joyous*. Your mind, body, and soul connection literally changes moment to moment with the thoughts and feelings that you hold. Try this right now. Think of a moment when you felt bad about yourself. You may have done something that you judged as *wrong* or *bad*. As you think about it now, notice your feelings inside as well as how your physical body responds. You may feel contracted, tense, or empty inside.

Now think of a moment when you felt on top of the world. You were happy with yourself. Put yourself back there in that moment and relive the thoughts and feelings. Recall how you felt about yourself. Feel how that feels in your mind and body. Notice what changes you experience as you shift from one experience to this other, higher experience. You just consciously changed your vibration.

Your Soul sends you information, encouragement, and practical guidance all the time. Your capacity to consciously tune in to this and capture its value is partly dependent on your vibration. As in the exercise above you can consciously choose where to focus and therefore raise your vibration.

Consciously Raising Vibration

Many external forms of nourishment and stimuli can assist in the conscious raising of vibration. I recommend that you start and end each day with some external form of stimuli that is at a higher vibration than your usual self. This may take the form of written materials such as a book, poetry, or meditation, or it may be recorded music, chanting, or inspirational speaking. At the start of the day and just as you are preparing for sleep, your mind is drifting down into alpha state. Your conscious and unconscious minds are connected more deeply, and brain waves cycle through at both levels at the same rate. This is when you are most suggestible and best able to be influenced by the higher vibrational words or sounds.

To be even more proactive you can identify the specific thoughts and feelings that pull your vibration down and choose nourishing materials with statements that focus on raising vibration in those areas. As a child, Sarina was constantly told she was stupid. Whenever she came across a challenging opportunity at work her inner voice reminded her to not get too confident because she was *stupid* after all. She tried to prove to herself and others that she was not stupid, but unconsciously she believed the childhood label to be true.

I worked with Sarina to raise her vibration in regard to her feelings about her intelligence. She did some regression work in the style I described in chapter 4. I recommended that she read materials that would focus her on the thoughts and feelings about herself that matched her desired goals. She chose some books to keep by her bedside that helped to raise her vibration towards more love and respect of herself. To influence her unconscious mind we created and taped a personal recording of her own voice affirming those qualities she wished to express and own. Today she is closer than ever to her goal of being a self-employed trainer and consultant.

Many people ask me how they can affect their feelings. "Aren't feelings just feelings?" they ask. No, feelings are a result of how you're choosing to be. You can transform how you feel about anything by choosing how you wish to be in the world. Feelings are a message from your soul—moving you to choose a way to be so that you will feel the way you choose to feel. So, if you choose to feel fulfilled, happy, and on purpose, then choose to be happy, fulfilled and on purpose, and follow the inspiration that comes from that.

Let me repeat these steps more clearly. Choose how you wish to be. For example, happy, fulfilled, on purpose. Ask for that by connecting to your Higher Self and stating that this is your request. Allow others to help you fully understand the meanings of the inner and outer messages. Follow, absolutely, the guidance that comes back to you, with faith and trust. Choose to focus your mind, body, and feelings on those higher vibrational ways of being that are magnetic to what you're choosing. Your feelings will begin to match the vibration of the higher way of being that you've chosen.

Conscious, Proactive Healing

One of the fastest routes to vibrational increase is through conscious healing. This requires that you do three things well:

(1) Track those areas of your life where you feel stuck, upset, off balance or unsatisfied. (2) In those areas, set a goal for how you would like things to be. You don't need to be specific about outcomes; it's enough to be specific about how you choose to feel. (3) Be willing to change. This may require the letting go of things you have held dearly up to now—thoughts, feelings, ways of being. Then ask your soul to help you heal, and to bring to you the love, support, people or situations that will allow that healing to unfold with grace.

This may mean that you seek the assistance of a facilitator—a healer, therapist, mentor—or it may come to you through the experiences of life.

Jack knew that he was far from realizing his full potential. Inside he felt his Soul Purpose had something to do with educating others about mystical experiences. On the outside his occupations were usually in the field of electronics. He spent several years, on his own, uncovering life experiences that had led him away from his true nature. He felt ready to go deeper and knew he needed help from someone who could reflect his highest image back to him.

I felt Jack's emotional pain the moment he entered my office. His body was physically contracted around his heart centre, and his speech was hesitant and slow. He looked at me more from the corners of his eyes than straight ahead, as if he was unsure of how he would be received. Every sentence from his mouth included a negative statement about himself or life in general. He reacted with anger to any suggestions of ways he could present himself more positively to the world. He even attacked me for accepting payment for work that was supposed to be *spiritual*. As I listened I heard a little boy inside begging to find a way to be valued and accepted, yet certain that everyone's response to him would be rejection. (Jack is the boy from chapter 4, whose mother asked him to spell *turtle*.)

We built enough trust in each other to explore the reasons for his anger and fear. His childhood memories were predominantly about his mother telling him he was wrong when inside he knew he was right. Most painful were moments when he was being drilled on schoolwork and was told his answers were wrong, when they were actually correct. He couldn't pursue his Soul's Purpose as an adult because he felt crushed by the constant suppression of his true feelings and thoughts as a child.

Jack responded well to healing using regression as well as to coaching that helped him to express his positive traits to build friendships or succeed in job interviews. Through revisiting the past he realized that the decisions he had made about himself, life, and others were limited by his childhood perspective. Through the healing, he recreated his childhood responses and allowed in more unlimited beliefs. He was now moving closer to his Soul Purpose because he was back in touch with his own inner truth.

The other way in which you can bring your soul to Earth is by calling upon it for assistance in everyday life. Don't wait until the next crisis hits to develop a close relationship with your spirit. Ask for help with the mundane as well as the profound. If you can't get the tape dispenser to work just say, "Higher Self, help me to get some tape." If you're looking for a book at the store, ask your soul to find it for you quickly. You'll learn a lot about the ways spirit interacts just by asking and then watching to see what comes back.

When it comes to Soul Purpose, ask for lots of support from your soul. "What am I here to do? Show me a vision of my highest future. Guide me to the easiest path to find my life's purpose. Give me a clear message about the next steps on my path." Ask for it to come easily, clearly, and with practical support. If you don't understand the thoughts, feelings, or messages that come back to you, tell your soul to send it in a different way. Then be prepared to act on what shows up.

All Work Is Spiritual Work

When it comes right down to the essence of Soul Purpose, there are common themes for all of us. What truly makes each of us happy can be found somewhere on the list of Universal Energies in Appendix 1. You may then ask why each of us has a unique way of expressing those energies. Why aren't we all doing the same things? What we share is a fundamental purpose to express an aspect of God. What is unique in each of us is the aspect we *choose* to express and how.

If each of us is busy expressing an aspect of God, our own unique expression of Divine energy, then how can any form of work be anything less than spiritual? How is expressing Divine beauty through wood designs as a carpenter any less spiritual than the teachings of a priest? Who says that music, in any form, is any less spiritual than the work of a nun? Can driving a taxi be spiritual if that is the form of expression for your unique Soul Purpose? If we are spiritual beings in human form, how can anything we do be separated from spirit?

This is where the age-old confusion about spiritual work and money requires a new storyteller. I find that many people have difficulty connecting with their soul or their Soul Purpose because they believe that the work of the soul should be given freely. Somewhere in the mass consciousness is a fear that what we do for money must be ego-driven and what we do for the soul is driven by Divine Will. Please! Money is not inherently *bad*.

All work is spiritual work because there is nothing else but Divine energy. You can and will do your Soul Purpose and it's just and fine to receive fair monetary compensation for your efforts. Abundance is a Universal Energy. It is a Divine Right. You can be spiritually connected and acting in everyone's highest interests and be paid well for it. You can also claim to be spiritually driven and hold a selfish, purely ego-driven intent.

Just because you say you are doing the work of God doesn't mean your intent and ability to channel God's Will is pure. And, conversely, you can be the purest channel of Divine Will and use that energy to do something not obviously spiritual, such as write computer code.

In the end, the only story that holds power for me is that energy follows intent. If it is your intent to act in the highest interests of yourself and those around you, your actions will follow your best ability to do that. If your intent is out of alignment with your own soul it will most likely serve you and others poorly.

When it comes to Soul Purpose, be prepared to get on a fast track to testing your abilities to listen and follow through on the messages of your soul. This will bring you abundance because the Universe will absolutely support you in doing your purpose, including sending you the financial resources to stay on track. This may include having the money you require, and/or the support of friends, family, co-workers, or strangers.

EIGHT

Inspiration To Act On

Your Soul Purpose

SOUL PURPOSE is a lifelong pursuit requiring courage, persistence, and willingness to evolve. To stay on track you require constant inspiration and impeccable connection to yourself and your soul. The prayers, affirmations, self-hypnosis tools, and meditations in this chapter and in Appendices 2 and 3 have been designed to feed you on all levels and assist you in the connecting that will bring you closer to your dreams. Use them and adapt them to what works best for you.

Prayer

These prayers are designed to assist you in calling forward the spiritual assistance to clarify and actualize your Soul Purpose.

Prayers For Soul Purpose

A Call To Purpose

I call forward my Higher Self, my guides and teachers, and the Universal energies of the Mother, Father, God, and Universal Power. I open to your wisdom and guidance.

I ask for clear and specific guidance to fulfil my purpose with ease.

Bless me with the clarity, passion, and power to see who I am, to embrace my gifts and talents, and to trust my moments of joy. Send me clear insights about the actions I may take to create a life where I may do my purpose joyfully, easily, daily.

Mother, inspire me with awareness of my inner, intuitive thoughts and feelings.

Father, show me the actions I may take to align with my soul and give new birth to spirit in my life.

Divine Creator, thank you for giving me the gift of creativity, that I may design and manifest a life on purpose.

A Letter To God

Dear Creator, blessed friend and lifelong companion,

Send me a parcel of courage that I may believe I have a reason for being,

Send me the healing that I may believe I am worthy of a life on purpose,

Give me the humility to accept the circumstances of my purpose regardless of the bigness or smallness of my occupation,

Grant me the humour to see that I am you even when my purpose seems too small,

And, dear friend, help me to accept responsibility for navigating my life by the light of passion, joy, and desire.

Soul Purpose Affirmations

I am alive.

I am a human being.

I am a human being happy.

I choose happiness as my emotion of choice.

And I stay with happiness regardless of external circumstances.

I am master of my emotions, creator of my body and owner of my life.

I have a purpose.

My soul and I create it.

I easily connect to myself—my body, mind, heart, and soul.

I choose to be in my body, aware of myself, and conscious.

I use my consciousness to track my healing.

And I transform myself to live my Soul Purpose with joy and delight.

NINE

Closing Words

My hope is that this book has given you hope. Somewhere in the exercises, stories, and inspirational tools I believe you will have reconnected with the truth...

Whether you feel successful right now or not, you can always be more in touch with your Soul Purpose. There is always more abundance, more joy, more grace available.

We are spiritual beings in physical bodies. If you are choosing to have all areas of your life work, then choose to reconnect spiritually, choose to heal, and choose to be here, fully in your body.

It will require absolute willingness to know the truth, as well as absolute willingness to listen to your soul. The good news is that more and more people are choosing a higher path.

If you happen to be one of the brave souls who is working on your healing while living in a traditional, corporate environment,

> *We all have a purpose.*
> *Our soul is the*
> *purpose-keeper.*

> *You can get back in touch with your passion and purpose.*

you probably feel like a dolphin swimming amongst the sharks. Take heart. Other dolphins are nearby.

Every time you feel an impulse to change your life in any area, revisit *Soul Purpose*. Remember, creating your Soul Purpose is a lifetime job. You will know it is time to come back to the book and the principles when you feel disconnection or discontent.

Do not give up on your healing, even when it seems like the healing never ends. You will see the inner changes reflected in your outer life. After all, we each manifest our lives based on what is going on inside us.

> *More people are valuing spiritual connection over social convention.*

Although our lives have speeded up, the change of pace is a gift. It is forcing you to focus on what's meaningful. So do that. Let go of the rest. Focus on your Soul Purpose by looking for the moments that create happiness until you are able to create happiness in every moment. Reinvent yourself from the inside.

You can have your Soul Purpose and real world success. They are meant to go hand in hand. Many people have proven it to me. We are meant to experience joy—if we choose it.

Please share your joy and let me know how the book is working in your life. (You may contact me by e-mail at **janeta@infinity.net**) Inspire others by telling your story and encouraging their growth. Soul Purpose is about creating a life you will love. And, if we all join in that process together, we just may create a world we all love.

Appendices

Appendix 1

Universal Energies[10]

Abundance	Healing	Power
Balance	Honesty	Purification
Beauty	Hope	Purpose
Charity	Humility	Responsibility
Clarity	Humour	Service
Compassion	Inspiration	Simplicity
Courage	Joy	Spontaneity
Creativity	Light	Strength
Discernment	Love	Transformation
Faith	Obedience	Truth
Forgiveness	Oneness	Vitality
Freedom	Openness	Willingness
Grace	Order	
Gratitude	Patience	
Happiness	Peace	
Harmony	Play	

Appendix 2

Meditation for Reconnecting
to Your Body, Mind, Heart and Soul

This meditation was created to assist you in grounding your energies to the Earth while reconnecting to yourself on all levels and aligning with your soul. It is adapted from a meditation created by Gordon-Michael Scallion and Cynthia Keyes.[5] You may choose to use it each morning for 21 days to wire it in your cells. After 21 days, use it 2 – 3 times a week as a way of maintaining your connections. Enjoy it inside or outdoors and have fun with various plants, trees, rocks and crystals.

Sit comfortably on the floor with a plant and a rock or crystal. These can be any size or species; just pick those that appeal to you. Place yourself, the plant, and rock in the shape of a triangle with each of the three at an apex of the triangle. Close your eyes and imagine a beam of light travelling up your spine and going all the way up to the spiritual level (or Heaven), as far as you can imagine. Then, see the beam coming back down and separating into three beams, each one striking one of the three objects (you, the plant, and the rock). Imagine the beams forming the sides of a huge triangle with the apex touching Heaven; and you, the rock, and plant forming the three corners of the base.

Then, imagine the three beams continuing down through the Earth and joining at the centre or core of the Earth. In your mind, see the beams of light forming a large diamond with the top apex touching Heaven, the bottom apex touching the core of the Earth, and the points in the centre touching you, the plant, and the rock. Open yourself to feeling your connection to spirit, the Earth, your body, mind, and heart.

Appendix 3

Self-Hypnosis Meditation Transcript

The most powerful way to use this transcript is to record it, in your own voice, and play it just before you go to sleep and/or just as you awaken in the morning. This is when your brain is most likely to be in alpha state and therefore most open to suggestion.

You may want to add background music as you are recording. Choose something soothing and heart-opening. Enjoy the meditation and feel free to adapt it to include your *Energetic-of-Soul Purpose*. You'll see where you can insert it below. Adapt the transcript first by writing in your Universal Energies and *Energetic-of-Soul Purpose*. Then, you're ready to record.

There are several spots where you may pause and let the tape run as you are recording, to leave space on the tape for you to reflect in the moment.

Here is the transcript:

I allow my mind to slip into relaxation. I let go of any thoughts and focus my mind on only these words. I allow all other thoughts to fade away and dissolve. The more I listen to this tape the more my mind hears only these words.

I allow my whole body to relax, as if I am resting in the arms of My Higher Self. I give My Higher Self all of my body and mind to hold and comfort. I ask My Higher Self to hold me tenderly and gently as my whole body relaxes.

I take my awareness to my feet. I feel the weight of my feet pressing down. I contract the muscles of my feet and scrunch my toes. I hold, scrunch, and relax...letting go of any tension in my feet. Now I focus on my legs and thighs...and feel their weight. I tense the muscles in my legs and thighs. I tense, and hold...and now relax my legs totally. I allow them to drop down towards the Earth as I am held safely in the arms of My Higher Self.

I bring my mind to my arms and feel their heaviness. I tense my arms and make fists with my hands. I hold the tension, and then...let go...allowing my arms to totally relax. I spread my fingers, as my hands release any tension and melt. Focusing on my abdomen, I tense my abdominal muscles, squeeze them tight, and now...I relax my abdomen completely...feeling it soften and let go. I feel my whole body relax and let go. With every breath I feel more and more relaxed.

I feel my chest and shoulders. I tense my shoulder blades together and squeeze the muscles, holding...and then relaxing. I let go of my shoulders and feel them fall into deep relaxation. I feel all of my body relax more and more. My mind is still empty and focused only on these words. I stay in the moment and relax.

I bring my awareness to my face, feeling my forehead, jaw, and neck. I tense the muscles in my face, squint my eyes and clench my jaw. And then...I relax. I feel my face soften, and let my jaw open slowly. I relax my eyes and forehead. I can feel my whole body relax and melt gently into the arms of My Higher Self. I allow My Higher Self to take the full weight of my body and mind. I let go and let My Higher Self take over...as I relax. Every breath feels more and more relaxing.

As I count backwards from ten to one, I fall into deep relaxation...letting go of fatigue, tension, and stress...and opening to peace and stillness.
Ten—drifting down into relaxation, relaxing physically...
Nine—relaxing more deeply and completely...
Eight—my muscles are relaxing and letting go...

Seven—every number takes me deeper as I relax mentally...
Six—the deeper I go, the easier it is to relax...
Five—connecting to My Higher Self...
Four—as I breathe deeper and deeper my body is letting go...
Three—drifting down into total relaxation, letting go of emotions...
Two—letting go on every level...
One—I am feeling very relaxed and at peace, resting in the arms of My Higher Self...

I imagine now that I am walking with My Higher Self in a beautiful forest. It is a warm, sunny day, and I feel the heat of the sun on my forehead. There is a cooling breeze that feels refreshing and invigorating. I have endless energy, joy, and peace, in my mind, body, and heart. I am my perfect, whole self. As I walk along I notice squirrels scurrying over the ground, birds singing in the trees, and butterflies drifting above the bushes. I allow my mind and body to go there and feel the forest. I notice a path ahead of me and follow it through the woods. It feels safe and inviting. I am escorted by My Higher Self and feel its loving presence.

I see a house ahead of me on the path. I feel drawn to go there and it feels safe and comforting. I make my way to the house and notice that I feel more and more drawn to it, the closer I get. I come to the front of the house and walk up the steps to the front door. I am happy to be going into the house. It feels like a safe place to be. I open the door and step inside, closing the door behind me.

As I enter the front hallway I notice that it is filled with light. I feel My Higher Self beside me, encouraging me to keep going. I walk through the hallway and notice a door to my right. I open the door and step into a beautiful room, closing the door behind me. As I enter the room I am struck by the familiarity of the furniture and objects around me. I realize that this room has been created just for me. It has the art, colours, textures, furniture and decorations that perfectly match my taste. I notice small familiar items on the tables and smile as I realize that this room holds many reminders of the things I love.

(Create a period of silence on the tape so you can take some time to imagine the room and how you feel being there.)

I imagine myself sitting in a chair and feeling comfortable and relaxed. I imagine a large white screen in front of me. This is the screen of my creative imagination. I see and feel myself on the screen as I am right now. I realize I have the power and freedom to experience anything I wish. I use my creative mind to move through time and space...

I imagine I am floating up to a timeline above my head. I reach the timeline and travel forward to one year from today. I float down and drop into my life one year in the future.

I am now closer to my Soul Purpose and I stay connected to my body, mind, heart, and soul. I love and care for my body and take it into environments where my purpose may be manifested. I focus my mind on affirming those thoughts that are in alignment with my purpose. I choose to focus on the feelings that uplift me emotionally.

My body retains more energy and vitality as I focus my mind on my purpose. The only thoughts that stay in my mind are ones of a higher vibration, taking me closer to connection with my soul. All negative thoughts disappear.

I have more energy and more focus on creating a life of _____ . (Insert the Universal Energy here that reflects what you choose to create.) *The more I focus on positive thoughts, the more my body responds with health, energy, and higher emotions.*

I imagine all of the joy and vitality I'll experience by focusing on my Soul Purpose. I feel my body responding as if I am there right now...

(Leave another period of silence on the tape to imagine yourself being in your *Energetic-of-Soul Purpose*. Imagine the physical, emotional, mental, and spiritual levels of the experience.)

*I imagine loving myself and giving myself every opportunity to be in my **Energetic-of-Soul Purpose**. I realize that I don't have to leave my current situation to raise my vibration. I stay in tune easily with my physical body and what it is experiencing. I am aware of my thoughts, and work towards raising these thoughts to a higher level. I feel my emotions and do my healing so they may transform into higher, more loving emotions. I tune in to my soul and listen for guidance and insight. Through conscious intent, staying in my body and choosing to heal, I transform myself right now and therefore change my experiences.*

I relax my body and mind, and open to the voice of My Higher Self as I affirm the ideas that are in my highest interest. I let my mind fill with positive thoughts and I capture these thoughts easily, fully, and completely. Soon these loving thoughts fill my mind more and more.

*My whole being responds to the word **purpose**. I go deeper and deeper whenever I think, hear, or say the word **purpose**. I feel relaxed and still, opening to loving thoughts and positive ideas.*

I am easily able to focus my mind on loving thoughts. My mind is under my control and it responds with thoughts that bring me peace.

I easily focus on my purpose. I feel the loving presence of My Higher Self and relax, knowing that I am safe.

When something happens that used to take me away from my centre, I simply focus my mind on my purpose and remain calm. I use my creative mind to focus on the future I choose to create.

I feel My Higher Self's love and believe in its wisdom. I trust that everything will be taken care of...all of my needs will always be met.

*My being responds to the word **purpose**. Whenever I think, hear, or say the word **purpose**, it allows me to go deeper. I feel relaxed and still as I open to more physical energy, more loving emotions, and more positive, self-affirming thoughts.*

I feel myself there, experiencing my most fulfilling, joyous moments. I am connected on all levels, totally in tune with my soul and myself. I feel myself smiling as I talk to friends and tell them how well I am doing and how far I have come. I feel my mind working with loving thoughts, helping me to heal and evolve easily and quickly.

I choose to have my life evolve towards more joy, and I indicate that choice to myself right now by placing my hand on my heart...

(Create another silence to allow time to place your hand on your heart and to open yourself to feel joy.)

I use my personal power to focus my mind on what I choose to create. My mind focuses on love and hope. My mind easily lets go of fear and doubt. I move forward with absolute confidence in the safety of the future. My mind easily focuses on the outcomes I choose to create.

I choose to imagine a life where I am fulfilling my Soul Purpose. I choose happiness, fulfilment, and ease. My body chooses relaxation over tension. My mind chooses loving thoughts over thoughts of fear. I focus on emotions that are loving, powerful and strong.

I fully own my creative power. The more I use it, the stronger it becomes. I imagine using my creative power right now. I imagine a situation where I once felt limited and unfulfilled...

(Create another space to imagine a situation where you felt limited and unfulfilled.)

Now I place my hand on my heart and focus on my purpose. I CHOOSE *to imagine this situation transforming. I see myself using my creative powers to change myself and therefore attract a new, unlimited situation. I imagine it coming to me without any effort. Just as I require anything, I imagine it coming right to me. I choose the new situation because I am focused on my purpose and sure of my happiness.*

I am closer to my soul in every moment. My conscious and unconscious minds are easily storing these thoughts. I love myself and easily change to be more loving and fulfilled. (You can replace these words on your tape with ones that more closely fit your *energetic.*) *I open to the gifts of my soul. I am now aligning with my soul to create my life with more ease and grace. My life is already improving as I take in these thoughts and make them my own.*

The new-found joy and positive thoughts become so much more attractive on every level. I now easily accept that I have a purpose and I am attracting the circumstances to live that purpose every day. Every time I see, hear, or say the word **purpose***, these suggestions go deeper into my cells.*

Now I pause, hold my hand on my heart, and take in a deep breath. As I breathe out I relax my body. I imagine my future once again. I see myself smiling and strong.

(Create another silence to imagine being in your *Energetic-of-Soul Purpose*.)

I imagine the power and energy in every cell of my body. As I imagine my future, all of these suggestions go deeper and deeper into my cellular memory, becoming part of me. Simply because I choose to be in alignment with my purpose, it is so.

In a moment it will be time to come back to the present, back into my body on all levels.

(Pause)

On the count of five I will come all the way back into my body, feeling present, refreshed, fully awake, and centred.

One...I feel myself slowly and calmly returning to full awareness.

Two...every cell in my body is energized and refreshed.

Three...all of my muscles are relaxed and loose...I feel very good.

Four...my head feels clear and centred...I am mentally alert, physically strong and grounded, and emotionally strong.

On the number five, my eyelids open and I am connected to my body, and feel relaxed and focused.

Five...my eyelids are now open. I am fully present, relaxed, calm, open, and centred. Slowly, I take in a deep, soothing breath...stretch...and then relax.

References Cited

1. Roman, Sanaya & Duane Packer. *Creating Money: Keys to Abundance*. Tiburon: H.J. Kramer, 1988. (This book is about using spiritual principles to do what you love.)
2. Walsch, Neale Donald. *Conversations with God: Books 1 – 3*. New York: G.P. Putnam, 1995, 1997, 1998. (Fabulous books to help you reconnect spiritually.)
3. Walsch, Neale Donald. *Friendship with God*. New York: G.P. Putnam, 1999. (The title says it all—what better way to build your spiritual connection?)
4. Pert, Candace. *Molecules of Emotion*. New York: Touchstone, 1997. (A new way to understand the mind-body connection through our biochemistry.)
5. Scallion, Gordon-Michael & Cynthia Keyes. *The Earth Changes Report*, a monthly newsletter. New Hampshire: The Matrix Institute, monthly.
6. Anand, Margo. *The Art of Sexual Ecstasy*. New York: J. P. Tarcher, 1989. (A good book to introduce you to some simple tantra exercises for getting in touch with sexual energy in your body.)
7. Liu, Dr. Hong & Paul Perry. *Mastering Miracles*. New York: Warner Books, 1997. (An inspiring story of the practice of Qi Gong and some simple exercises to use for health and grounding.)
8. Gawain, Shakti. *Creative Visualization*. New York: Bantam Books, 1978.
9. Lozoff, Bo. *It's a Meaningful Life—It Just Takes Practice*. New York: Penguin Books, 2000. (This book has inspiring ideas for consciously bringing meaning into your life.)
10. Huffines, LaUna. *Bridge of Light: Tools of Light for Spiritual Transformation*. Tiburon: H. J. Kramer, 1993. (A practical guide for connecting to the Universal Energies mentioned in *Soul Purpose*.

LaUna calls them "soul qualities.") For a more complete understanding of Universal Energies, refer to the many books on angels which discuss these soul qualities. The "Angel Cards," created at the Findhorn Foundation, copyright 1981 by Drake & Tyler, are a great tool to encourage connection with these energies.

11. Hill, Napoleon. *Think and Grow Rich*. New York: Ballantine Books, 1960. (One of the first books to teach the universal principles of manifesting.)

12. Stearn, Jess. *The Power of Alpha-Thinking*. New York: William Morrow & Co., 1976. (Some simple, powerful meditations for

Contacting The Author

Now that you've read *Soul Purpose*, please stay in touch. Janet Amare is currently at work on her next book and would love to hear your stories. Janet's business, *Soul Purpose Inc.*, provides coaching, healing, retreats and seminars to help you create your life in alignment with your purpose. Personal coaching and healing are offered by phone or in person, to clients all across North America.

Find out more about products and services by browsing the website at **www.mysoulpurpose.net**. You can send an e-mail through the site, or write to the address below:

Soul Purpose Inc.
P.O. Box 542
Campbellville, Ontario L0P 1B0
CANADA